Acrylics
from scratch

ART WORKSHOP WITH
PAUL TAGGART

Acrylics
from scratch

Art Workshop with Paul

Paul Taggart

Series Concept and Structure by Eileen Tunnell
Series Design and Layout by Sunita Gahir
A **QUILLS MEDIA** PRODUCTION WWW.QUILLSMEDIA.COM

First Published in Great Britain in 2006 by
Sandcastle Books Limited
The Stables
Sheriffs Lench Court
Sheriffs Lench
Nr. Evesham
Worcs. WR11 4SN

www.sandcastlebooks.co.uk

ISBN 0-9552478-2-9

Printed and bound in Thailand

Contents

Acrylics

Acrylic is a versatile and dynamic medium, whose beauty is reliant on its strength of character and finish. When fully exploited, it offers a wealth of possibilities and a limitless range of techniques, to suit painters of any level. Not surprising therefore, that acrylics paints have become so popular, with children and adults alike, since their introduction.

The principles of acrylic painting *can take you on a journey from the simplest of coloured daubs, through to highly detailed, photo-realistic renditions. This range of capabilities makes it attractive not only to the would-be adult painter, but also to the professional artist.*

Acrylic painting is a modern medium and one that is unique; it is quite unlike any of the other media, such as watercolours, oils and pastels. However and contrary to the general view, it is not restricted to a modern approach, for it can be exploited to achieve results that are based on many of the traditional techniques used in watercolour, oil and pastel painting.

Delicate miniatures on gesso panels, formal portraits on canvas, gentle Line and Wash sketches on watercolour paper, landscapes carried out in the manner of Wet on Wet and Wet on Dry watercolours, or that of bold brushy oil paintings.

A riot of textures in a rural landscape prove irresistible as a means of exploiting brush-strokes on pages 74 to 77.

***The principles of Acrylic From Scratch** will introduce you to the world of painting in acrylics, using a starter set of materials and painting tools. The opening section covers the basics of these materials and is followed by the guiding principles in colour mixing, which leads you logically into a series of projects.*

There are many exercises and practice pieces, plus stage-by-stage paintings for you to follow. These will require time and patience and should be carried out at a leisurely pace. Nothing will give you greater pleasure and a sense of achievement than seeing an improvement in a simple exercise that has been frequently practised.

This book includes numerous exercises to help you become familiar with your tools and others in which to become familiar with a variety of techniques. The tutorials are meant as guides, not as finished paintings that you should slavishly follow to produce exact copies.

Brightly coloured boats bobbing about on the sun-drenched water of a Mediterranean harbour are used to exploit palettes mixing to its fullest on pages 82 to 85.

When carrying out the exercise and tutorials, your results need not be perfect. Instead, expect to learn something new each time you carry them out.

Unfortunately muddy colours are a common problem for painters and can be easily avoided. The solution lies in a basic understanding of colour and the secret is a simple approach to colour mixing,

Initially, concentrate on the various exercises; work on these until you feel comfortable with the basic technique covered in any particular one. At that point move on to the relevant stage-by-stage painting and you are more likely to gain from the experience.

The stage-by-stage paintings are included to provide you with the inspiration to develop and are challenging. Do not expect instant results, nor should you strive to produce exact replicas. It is the process that matters, not the end result and it is your successful development that will prove far more fulfilling.

All too often, enthusiastic would-be painters find themselves deeply frustrated and more often than not blame their own inadequacies. In my experience, this is rarely the case and is usually rectified through ensuring the painter has access to the necessary instruction and information.

Acrylics From Scratch is meant as a sound introduction to acrylic painting for beginners and those returning to painting. It should also prove a useful refresher to those who already paint, providing them with some new approaches.

A tactile surface for a tactile subject, the beauty of each brought into focus on pages 90 to 93.

Which paints do I need?

A simple, yet essential question, which needs to be addressed before you begin to gather a collection of materials for your journey into acrylic painting.

It would seem that acrylic paints are to be found in a plethora of guises these days, one of the most familiar being household decorating paints. What exactly is the difference between these and acrylic paints used to create paintings?

THE TWO PRIMARY INGREDIENTS in any paint are pigment (the colour) and medium (the glue). Pigment, generally a coloured powder, needs a method by which it can stick to the surface. In watercolours this medium is a gum, whereas in oil paints it is oil.

Acrylic paints are a little different, in that the medium is an emulsion, or fluid mix of a form of plastic combined with water. As long as the water is present, the plastic can flow. However, as soon as the water evaporates off, the plastic particles bind together and cannot be separated. The resultant plasticized film provides a very powerful and permanent layer, in which the pigment is trapped.

The difference in the qualities of paint depends largely on the type and amount of pigment in the paint mix. Pure pigment is expensive and can be extended with filler, or chalk, to make the paint cheaper. Chemical dyes also exist, which replicate pigment colours and these too can be less expensive, although not necessarily substandard to pigment.

Thus it is that various qualities of acrylic paint exist, such as household paints and acrylics specifically manufactured for a variety of hobby uses. For painters a wide range of qualities meets the needs of different applications, ranging from those used by children in schools, through to those available to artists, such as Students' Quality and Artists' Quality.

Generally, the better quality paints contain more pigment, resulting in colours that are more intense and when mixed, will give much purer results. Often, the more pigment in a paint, the more lightfast it will be, but each pigment also has differing degrees of permanency.

Therefore, although it is quite possible to produce paintings using household paints, their relative qualities and nature have to be taken into account.

Uncapping a tube of artist's acrylic paints for the first time introduces you to a paint that has a different feel to any other media. At first glance the colours seem to be very bright and slightly garish. This is due to the medium in the colour, which is white, while wet. However, the transluscent white fades to be wholly transparent, once the paint has dried, with the colour reverting back to the richness of the original pigment.

The consistency of acrylic paint lies somewhere between that of watercolour and oil, which allows the artist to work with it in fluid form, or in a stiffer mix. It does however possess a natural quality all of its own and never goes quite as thin as watercolours, or as stiff as oils.

Above all, to work with acrylic paints is to work with one of the strongest and most versatile of all painting media.

SELECTING YOUR PAINTS

Artists' Quality paints often vary in price between colours and this is simply due to the differing costs of the pigments, which in some cases are harder to obtain. It is important to be aware that a more expensive colour is not necessarily better, nor does the price indicate that it may be longer lasting. All Artists' Quality paints are given a rating system by each manufacturer, which denotes the fugitive nature of any individual colour.

Should you already possess some water-based paints, such as gouache or watercolours, these can be used to start you off. With the addition of either acrylic medium, acrylizing medium to the colour mixes, you will in effect be turning these into acrylic paint mixes. Although this will not result in as powerful colours as true acrylic paints, it will give you a feel for the medium, before investing further.

Understanding paints

Basic nature

In tubes of acrylic paint, the pigment (colour) is held in suspension in an emulsion (mix) of medium (glue) and water.

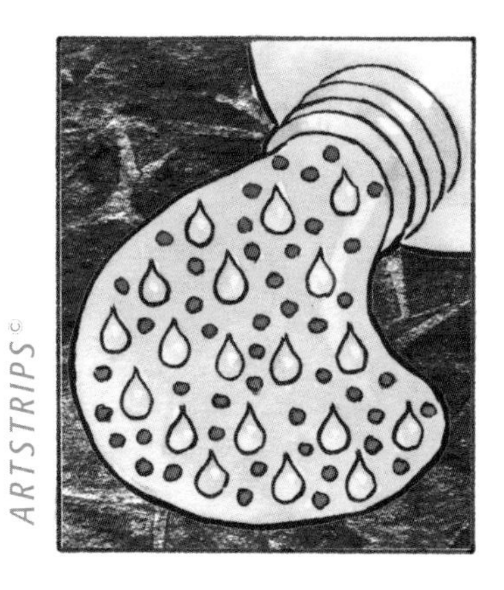

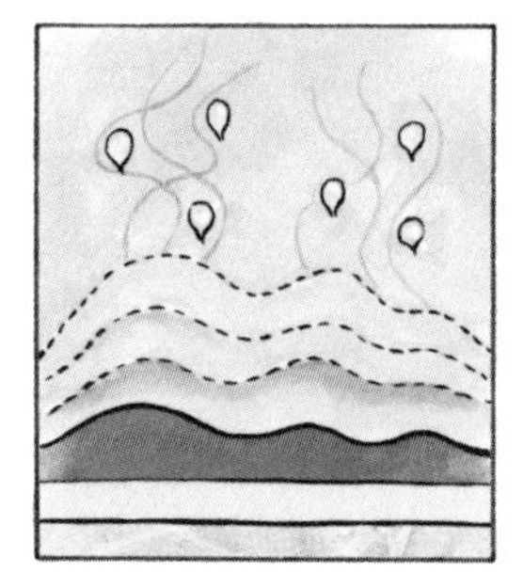

As soon as acrylic paint is exposed to the air the water evaporates, the paint shrinks and the medium hardens – encapsulating the pigment in a plastic film.

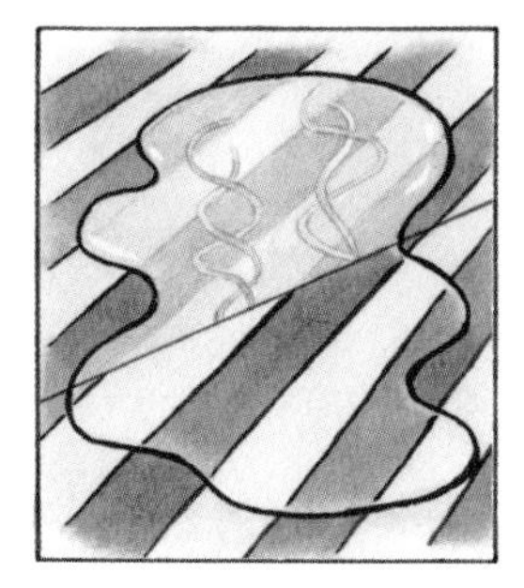

In wet paint the medium is translucent white. As soon as the paint dries, the medium turns from opaque to transparent.

Basic characteristic

Consequently, acrylic paint is lighter and more opaque when wet – but dries darker, richer and more transparent.

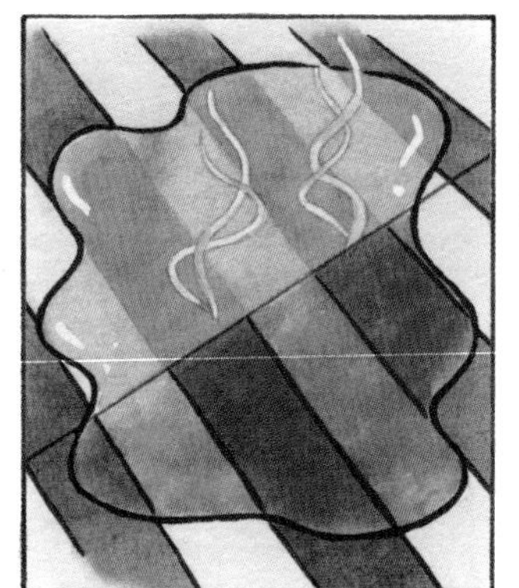

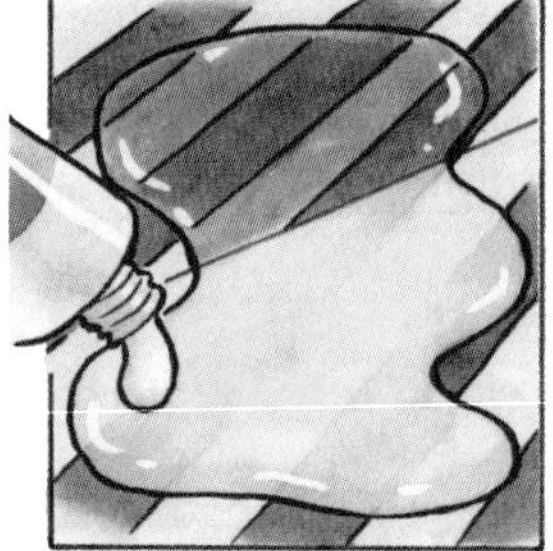

MIXES With the addition of white, the colour becomes lighter, duller and more opaque – when wet and when dry.

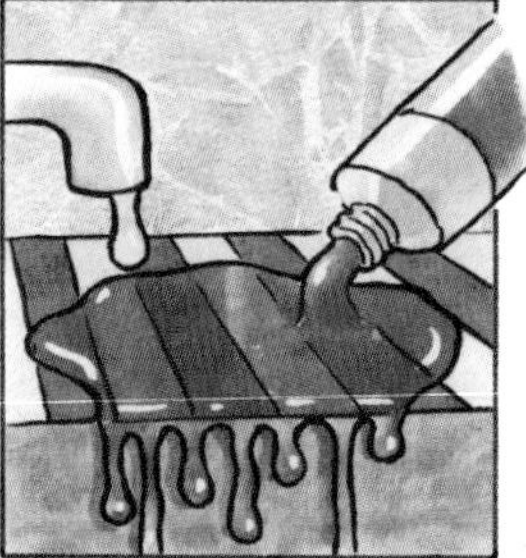

SOLUTIONS With the addition of water the colour becomes fluid and more transparent.

WATERCOLOUR PAINTING TECHNIQUES APPLIED TO ACRYLICS.

Since acrylic medium is water-soluble, it is quite possible to employ many of the fluid techniques from watercolour painting. Acrylics are, however, a completely different medium and it is important to understand their strengths in order to get the best out of them.

Acrylic paints produce transparent fluid washes of colour. While wet, they can be reworked, lifting colour out of the washes and/or adding colour to them. Brushing thin or thick colour into a wet layer will render soft, unfocussed edges, which could suggest depth and/or movement. When thin colour is applied to dry paper, it is possible to lose edges to create volume, or scuff the brush-strokes to invoke texture.

While these techniques are all similar to watercolours, the differences between the two media need to be understood, to fully appreciate the additional possibilities that working in acrylics has to offer. Acrylic colours darken as they dry and become richer, as opposed to watercolours, which lighten and become duller.

Colour washes are more easily overlaid in acrylic, since each layer dries to a permanent finish, as opposed to watercolours, where previously laid washes lift off. And finally, the use of white in acrylic, making the paint opaque and improving its covering power.

Mediums

The addition of extra medium makes the colour transparent – but quite viscous.

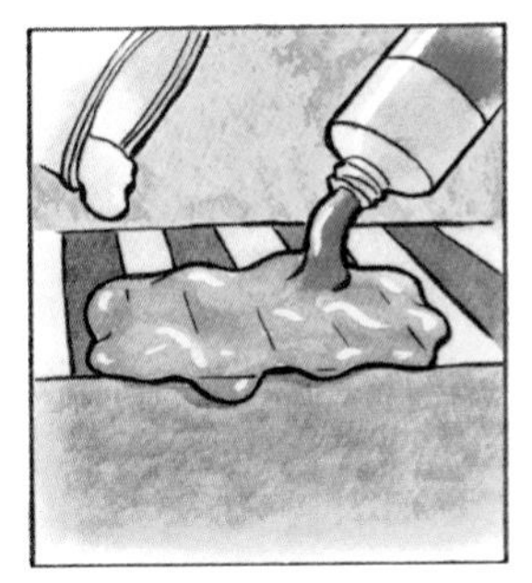

Gel mediums make the colour transparent – but gelatinous.

Texture/modelling paste makes the colour more opaque while retaining its intensity. The paint mix becomes stiff, making it suitable for impasto.

TIP
Simply add a small quantity of white to transparent glazes, to produce semi-transparent tints.

Application

WET ON WET
Paint is applied fluidly, or stiffly, into a wet surface. Resultant paint strokes develop soft edges.

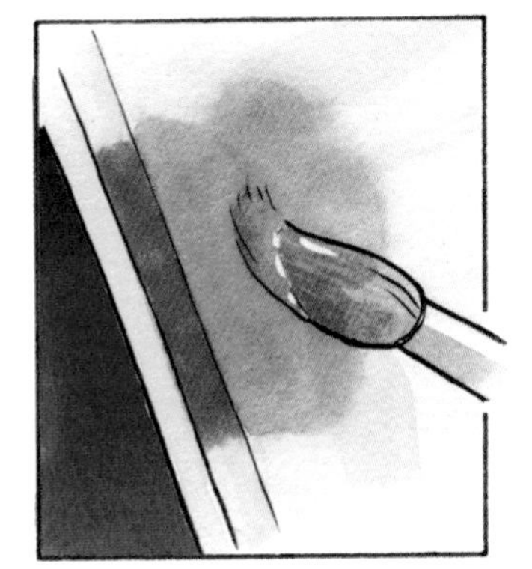

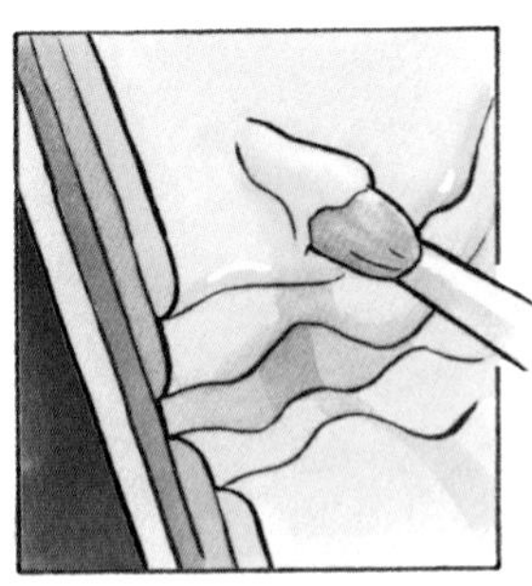

WET ON DRY
Paint is applied fluidly, or stiffly, onto a dry surface - building layers of sharp-edged strokes.

Thin solutions with water or mixes with medium (without white in either) create transparent glazes, or washes. These enrich and darken colours, or surfaces, beneath.

OIL PAINTING TECHNIQUES APPLIED TO ACRYLICS.

The addition of white to acrylics, thus creating opaque colours, along with the fact that impasto layers of colour can be created, allows for the use of oil painting techniques. Once again, however, although there are similarities, the different characteristics between these two media need to be taken into account.

Used opaquely, acrylic colour layers, thin or thick, are capable of covering each other quite easily. Nevertheless, broken or irregular surfaces are more interesting to the eye. Therefore, as the impasto layers are built, scuffing and scumbling of thick opaque overlays comes into play. Colour mixes themselves could be streaky and irregular, the heavy paint holding the colour variation as it dries. Once these impasto layers have dried, transparent layers of colour plus acrylic medium can be overlaid.

Whilst these techniques are common between oil painting and acrylic painting, there are differences. In acrylics the thick paint layers dry by evaporation and consequently lose some bulk through shrinkage. To compensate for this it is possible to add extra body, in the form of texture paste.

Acrylic colours dry darker and more transparent. This is something an acrylic painter quickly takes in their stride. The most important asset in painting with acrylics is the fact that it is fast drying. Impasto layers are soon ready for further work, as opposed to having to wait some time for them to dry, as you would in oil painting. Added to which, several layers of glaze can be applied in a fraction of the time.

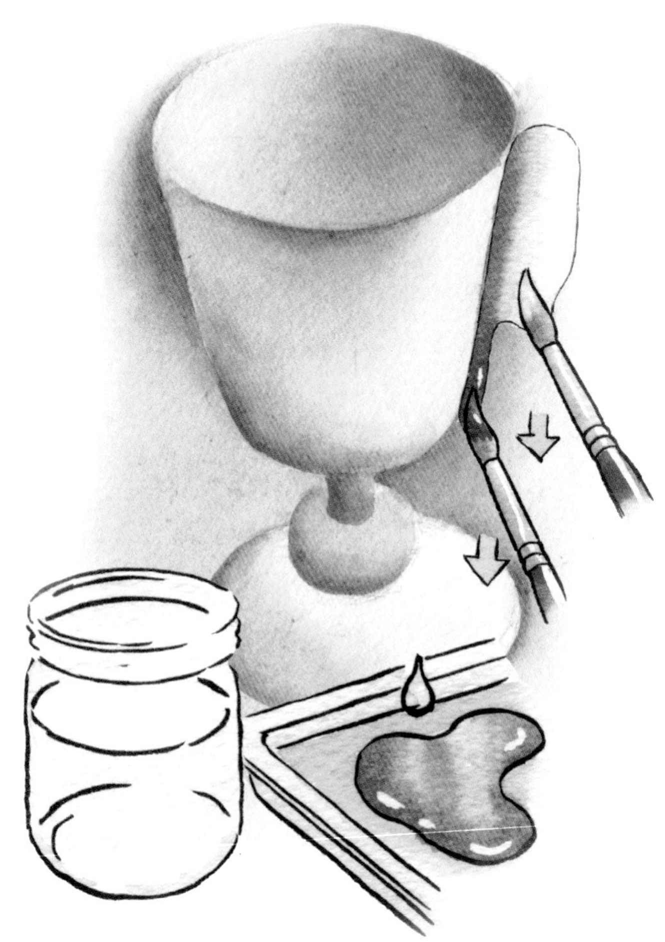

Paints in practice

Losing edges

Lost edges are created by depositing a fluid stroke of colour down the edge with one brush. A second, slightly larger brush is then used to wet the outside edge of the deposited colour, which runs into the wetted area – becomes lost. You can make the paint flow more easily in two ways. The first is to pre-wet the whole area, up to the edge that needs to remain hard; the second being to make the colour mix more fluid by adding extra water. In either case, the easier paint flow facilitates the softening of the edge to be lost.

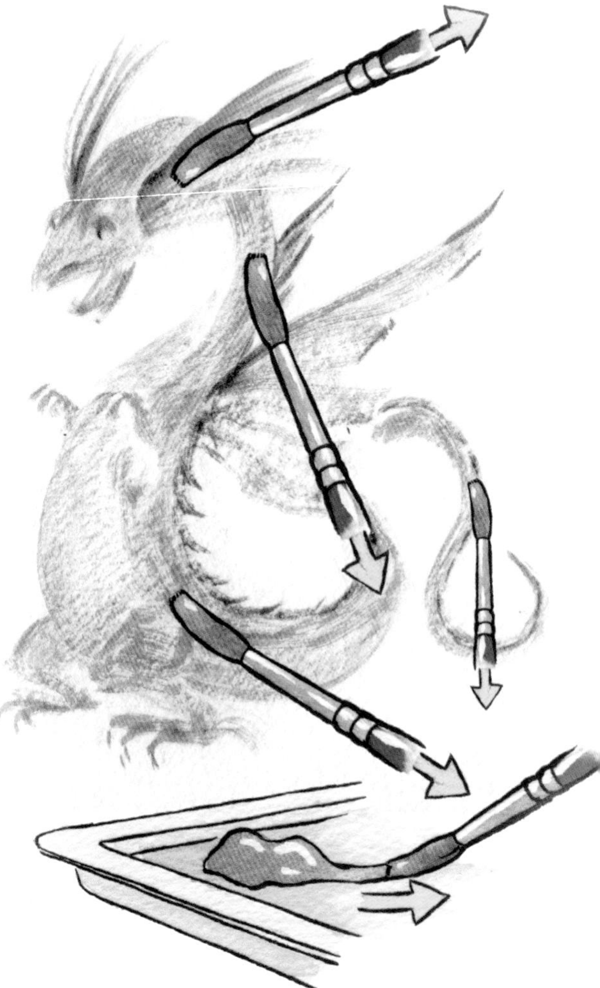

Scuffing and scumbling

Load the brush with stiffer paint and pull it across the palette to flatten its face. To apply, drag the brush in the direction of the required stroke, keeping the angle of the brush as close to the surface as possible. Follow the form of the subject with the brush, merely catching the uppermost textures of the paper, to leave an irregular deposit of paint. An individual stroke is referred to as a scuff and when scuffs are combined the technique is known as scumbling.

Wet on Wet - using water

This soft focus result is typical of the technique of Wet on Wet, which allows the viewer to imagine more than is actually portrayed. The surface is first thoroughly wetted with a Hake brush. The colour mix made fluid with the addition of a little water and applied with a round soft brush. The more fluid the mix, the more it will spread. As the surface begins to dry, work toward the main focal point (here the door opening), which becomes darker as a consequence.

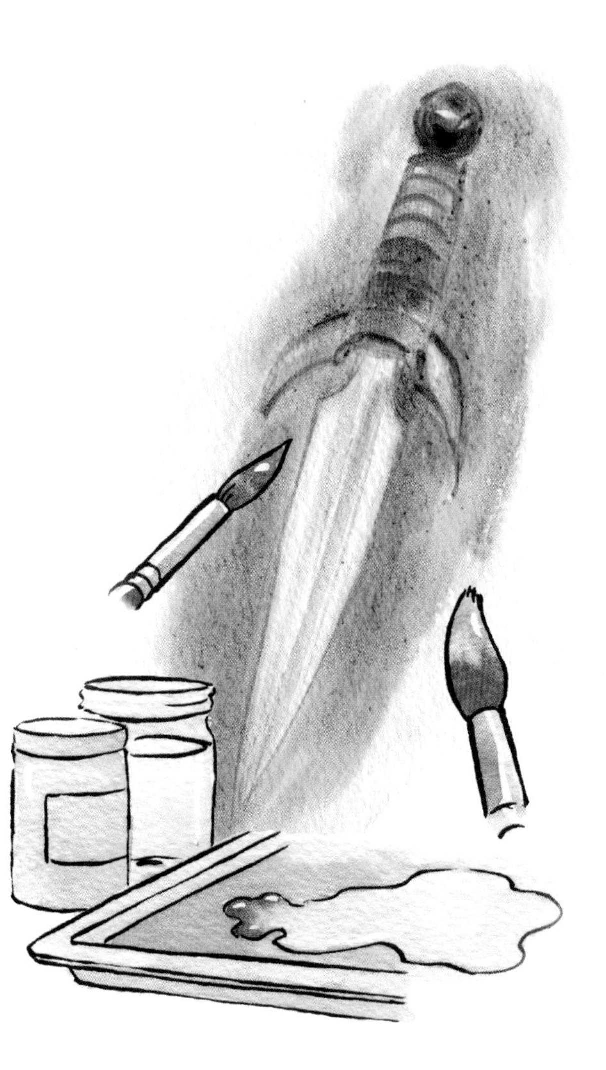

Wet on Wet - using medium

A pool of gloss medium, to which a little water has been added, is established on the palette surface. This is used to wet the surface and to make the colour mix more fluid. The surface is wetted with a large round soft brush; the colour with medium mix applied with a smaller round soft brush. The resultant strokes are much more stable, while still retaining the distinctive soft characteristics of the Wet on Wet technique.

Exercise for paints

Following an initial gentle pencil drawing, the main outline and features are described with a Rigger brush, loaded with a solution of black acrylic Indian ink. With a small round brush, stroke on masking fluid to protect highlights in the feathers. Do not over-load the brush with masking fluid and remove any excess by pulling the brush across the surface of the ceramic saucer palette.

Wet the surface liberally, using a Hake or large round brush. Create a fluid grey mix on the palette surface and load onto a large round soft brush. Apply wet-on-wet across the painting, beginning to softly suggest the form and solidity of the bird.

The study is now re-wetted in sections as you paint. Use the Hake brush to do this and the large round brush to deliver a succession of differing coloured greys, laying them wet-in-wet. Changing colour temperatures will excite the eye and in this instance the first grey to be applied was a yellow mixed with purple, the second a blue mixed with orange and the third a red-orange mixed with blue.

NOTE

ALTHOUGH ACRYLIC COLOURS CANNOT BE LIFTED ONCE DRY, THEY CAN BE OVERPAINTED WITH OPAQUE COLOUR, SHOULD ANY MISTAKES NEED RECTIFYING.

Use the same large round brush to now apply bright colour mixes using the Wet on Dry technique. Less water is added to the mix than previously. These strokes should be dragged and scuffed and will therefore be generally hard-edged. Use directional strokes to suggest the various characteristics of the feathers and the different directions in which they lie.

COMBINATION OF WATERCOLOUR TECHNIQUES

Throughout this study, colour mixes are applied as transparent layers, to show how watercolour techniques can be exploited with considerable ease. Transparent layers of fluid acrylic are every bit as beautiful as transparent washes of watercolour.

Whites and highlights are achieved with the use of masking fluid, not white paint. This technique with masking fluid is more generally associated with painting in watercolours. Although whites are available in acrylic painting to use over layers of colour, in this exercise, the paper itself is maximised to effect the whites and the highlights.

The final touch is a second application of the acrylic ink line-work, using a Rigger brush. The ink mix is well watered down, so that it does no dominate the subtle colours. Be loose and free with its application, adapting to the rhythms and general patterns of the feathers, rather than becoming too detailed and specific.

Why do I need a brush?

Since acrylic paint is probably the most versatile of all the painting mediums, it can equally be applied with a vast range of tools.

To achieve the more traditional methods of painting, such as those borrowed from watercolours and oils, specific brushes are needed to deliver specific techniques.

THE CHOICE OF BRUSHES for acrylic painting is entirely dependent on the manner in which the paint is to be applied and the desired result. If the paint is to be applied thickly, as in impasto painting, stiff bristle brushes are uniquely designed to cope with this.

Stiff bristle brushes, with their seemingly rigid hairs, are often intimidating for those new to painting. They appear clumsy and aggressive, but their power lies in this very strength of character. These brushes control stiff paint, creating textured strokes and building it up into layers. The bristle brush is therefore ideal for use with acrylic paint and even more so, when used for paint mixes that contain texture paste.

These stiff brushes are available in natural bristle, or their more modern equivalents, produced with nylon hairs.

Smoother application of paint requires brushes of a quite different nature and this is where the soft brush comes into its own. These also come in the form of natural hairs, such as sable, the most expensive of them all. Cheaper alternatives exist, offering painters a vast range of natural hairs to choose from, each having a quality of its own.

Nylon soft brushes have improved tremendously over the last few years and offer extremely worthwhile substitutes, especially for acrylic painters. Being stronger they tend to be longer lasting than natural haired brushes, especially when used over punishing surfaces such as dried acrylic impasto paint.

Of all the multitude of brush shapes on offer, the traditional round brush is by far the most versatile. Being round in cross-section it tends to point well, especially with the softer heads.

The round shape also holds a good supply of paint, enabling several strokes of colour to be made from a single loading. So versatile are they that an entire painting could be completed with round soft brushes alone, simply by employing different parts of the brush to fulfil different functions.

Although it is not essential to have any other brushes to progress in painting, it is helpful to try out other shapes as you develop. A useful brush to consider from the very start is the flat nylon brush. The strength of this shape lies in the fact that the flattened shape enables an even layer of colour to be delivered over the surface. This makes the flat nylon ideal for scuffing and scumbling, although it can be loaded more heavily to apply more succulent strokes.

For wetting large surface areas there is nothing to compare to the qualities of the Hake brush, particularly when it comes to working with the Wet on Wet technique. Since this watercolour technique is adaptable for use in acrylic painting, the Hake will prove invaluable for soft, atmospheric qualities.

Finally, the Rigger brush, which is best suited to line-work, for as its name implies, it was developed specifically for painting the rigging in sailing ships. This brush creates a far more responsive line than a pen or the point of a broader brush and helps in loosening up drawing and detail.

Although there are many more shapes and types of brushes that could prove interesting to you in the future, these five basic types form the nucleus of brushes used throughout the tutorials in this book.

COMMON TERMS

In Acrylics From Scratch I have standardised the terms applied to the use of brushes, in order to make things simpler for those new to painting.

The handle of a brush is known as the shaft. Traditionally made of wood with a sturdy coating, but plastic and other materials are also used these days

The hairs, or filaments, that make up the brush head are set into a ferrule, the collar that holds the brush head to the shaft. The hairs are most likely to be set into the ferrule with glue, which can soften when warmed. Generally this ferrule is made from metal, although in some specialist brushes other materials are used. Always wash brushes in cold or very tepid water, to prevent the metal ferrule from expanding and the glue softening, which would result in hairs falling out of the brush head.

In round brushes and the Rigger, the brush head makes two important contact points with the surface. The point being used for detail, while the side of the head – the shoulder – is employed for broader coverage.

In the case of flat brushes, the Hake and the flat wash brush, the tip of the brush is a long edge. The full edge is referred to as the tip, while one end of this edge is known as the corner of the tip.

The flat surface of the brush head is termed the face of the brush.

TIP:
When purchasing brushes, always opt for one that is two sizes larger than you originally thought. Larger brushes will offer as good a point as a smaller size and have the added benefit of holding more paint in any one loading to enable you to work on a larger area at any one time.

Understanding brushes

Although brushes specifically designed for acrylics are available, watercolour and oil painting brushes can also be used.

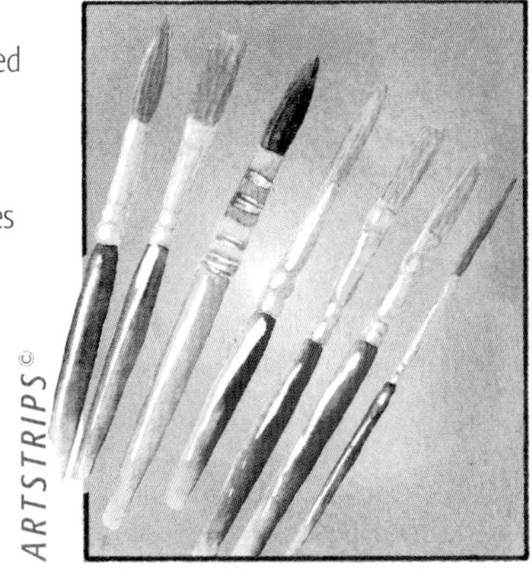

The deciding factor is if colour is to be applied like watercolour (top), or as stiff impasto, like oil painting (bottom).

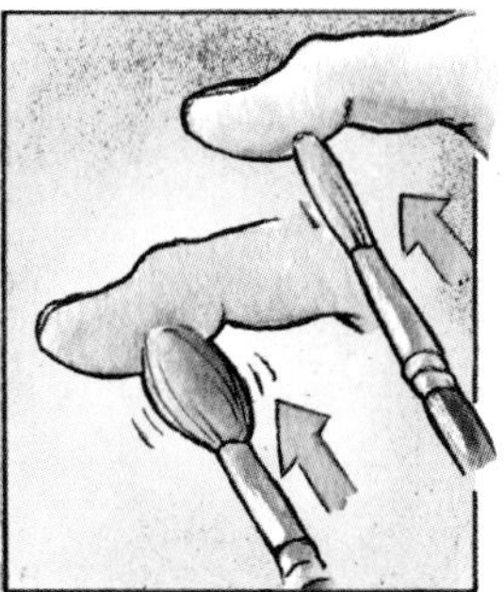

Soft brushes are traditionally made from natural hair, or nylon (bottom). The stiffer brushes from bristle (top).

Nylon brushes are now made to mimic the flexibility of natural hair (top), or the stiffness of bristle (bottom).

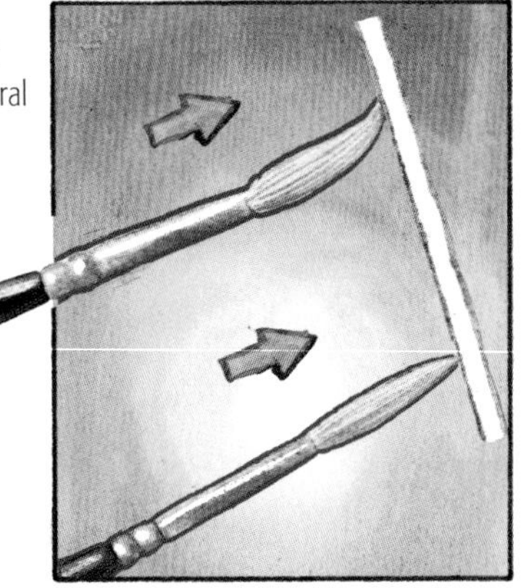

These have the advantage over soft natural hair since natural hair can easily damage when used to paint over dry impasto texture.

Stiff nylon brushes do not splay if left for too long in water, as would bristle brushes.

Since many techniques normally assigned to other media can be exploited in acrylic painting, it is reasonable to assume that brushes designed for those media are also suitable. Should you already possess watercolour or oil brushes, they can be made to work with acrylics.

However, nylon brushes possess a distinct advantage and in recent years considerable advances have been made in their manufacture. Mixes of nylon and natural hairs, such as sable, offer strength and flexibility.

Acrylic painting is one of the most punishing on brushes and even if care is taken not to let paint dry in the brush head, brush-strokes applied over dried acrylic surfaces cause damage. Little can be done about brush wear and tear, but the shape of the brush head can be maintained through correct care and proper storage. Never let a brush dry out of shape and after cleaning, carefully point or flatten the head back into its natural form.

TIP: To help restore a misshapen brush head, heavily impregnate the hairs with solid soap, as you reshape it. Let the soap dry in the head and store the brush until next required. On next using the brush, soften the soap in water for a few minutes and you will find that its shape will have improved. *Special soaps have been developed specifically for this purpose, if preferred.*

Overloading soft brushes with stiff colour causes bulking and loss of point (top). Instead, use stiff brushes for heavy paints (bottom).

SOFT ROUND BRUSH Versatile with fluid colour. The point is used for line-work, the shoulder for fast, even coverage.

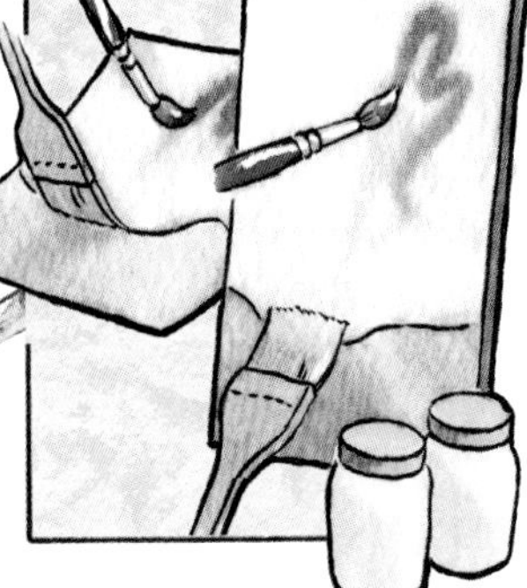

HAKE BRUSH Used to wet the surface with either water and/or medium when painting wet-on-wet.

RIGGER BRUSH Ideal for line-work and fine detail.

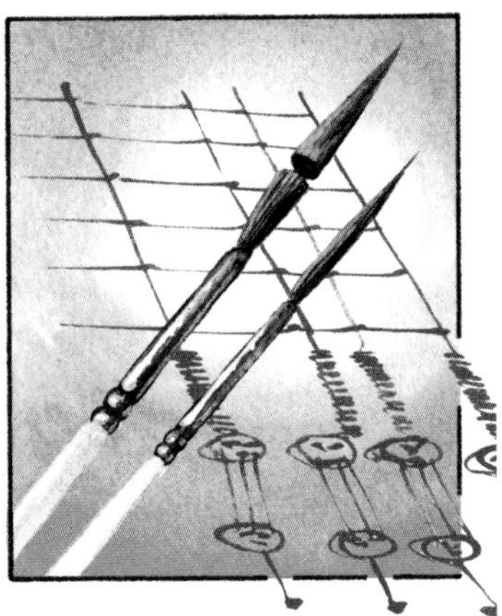

FLAT NYLON BRUSH Excellent for scuffing and scumbling to create broken paint layer over surface texture.

CAUTION Adequate paint flow through brush head reduces drying out. Frequently check base of hairs and ferrule for drying paint and clean brush thoroughly.

It is doubtful that any acrylic painter has not lost a brush through inadvertently allowing paint to dry in its head. It is easily done, even by professionals such as myself!

The medium in acrylic paint is incredibly strong and although this bodes well for the longevity of a painting, it does affect the life of brushes. Although medium can be thinned down by adding copious amounts of water, even the smallest amount left in a brush head will spell disaster.

Once the water has evaporated off, pure medium is left behind, which dries rock hard. This usually occurs right in the middle of the brush head, down towards the shaft. You may not be aware of it initially, the first hint being that the brush feels somewhat stiffer. This is the beginning of the end, for the small hard lump attracts more particles of paint and so it grows outwards from the centre, until the brush amounts to little more than a solid stick.

Be meticulous in cleaning every brush, do it once and take the precaution of doing it again. With a fingernail, gently massage some fluid soap down into the base interior of the brush head, then rinse and rinse again in cold water. Whilst this may seem tedious, it is nothing compared to the frustration and expense of losing brushes.

Brushes in practice

Hake and round soft brush

WET ON WET

This gentle, soft rendering takes advantage of the specific characteristics of two brushes. Use a Hake to wet the entire surface of a piece of stretched watercolour paper. This will ensure the brush-strokes that follow are soft-edged. All colour mixes are applied using a round soft brush. This technique, borrowed from watercolour painting, requires that colours are layered from light to dark. The consistency of colour mixes needs to therefore gradually thicken after the first thin fluid washes, to achieve the necessary contrasts. Using the Wet on Wet technique in acrylics has added advantages. First, once the paint has dried it can be rewetted without fear of previously laid colour lifting off. Second, opaque colours can be overlaid, such as the white strokes used to suggest the spines of the cactus.

Round stiff nylon/bristle brush

WET ON DRY

The watercolour paper surface is kept dry for this technique. The much stiffer hairs of the brush will deal with much heavier, stiffer paint. Before loading the brush with paint, dip it in water – this will slow down the speed at which paint dries in the brush head. However, take care not to allow any of this water to transfer to the paint mix, as this will reduce the body of the paint. To avoid this happening, gently squeeze the brush head in absorbent tissue to eliminate excess moisture. When loading your brush, dip it into the stiffer areas of the paint mix. Do not spread the mix too widely on the palette; instead build it into a mound to preserve its integrity.

In this instance layers are applied light to dark, before moving back to light colours.

Flat nylon brush

Since the surface quality has such an influence on the resultant strokes, you could consider varying this to the advantage of the end result. Watercolour paper was chosen for this study, so that the effect of the brushes could be compared on a like-for-like surface.

The flat nylon brush works equally well for general painting as it does for laying washes. However, its true strength lies in its ability to create scuffs and scumbles. The brush needs to be held very flat to the surface, so that it catches the prominences of the texture. Again, dampen and squeeze brush before loading with colour.

Paint mixes are kept as close to tube consistency as possible. However, the paint can be made stiffer or more transparent, with the addition of pastes, gels and mediums. This presents a vast array of possible scuff qualities, all of which you should explore.

Nylon rigger brush

The nylon Rigger is a brush designed for line-work. To produce the necessary responsive, descriptive line, the paint mix must be made as fluid as possible. Add water, along with a little medium to retain its strength of colour.

The instinctive response to the addition of line in a painting is to use it to strengthen outlines. However, line-work can be much more exciting and varied and the rigger brush is the one to achieve this.

Keep to the same size of brush for this exercise and concentrate on manipulating the brush head in different ways to achieve variety. In this instance, the brush head was pulled, pushed, swiped and dragged across the surface.

Bear in mind, that with acrylics, you can overlay light lines within dark areas, which offers further possibilities.

Exercise for brushes

2 Round stiff nylon/bristle brush
Re-wet the area of the flower head and immediately around it. Apply thicker strokes of colour with the stiff nylon, or bristle, brush. Note the partially mixed state of the streaky colour and how individual brush hairs create texture with each stroke.

1 Hake and round soft brush On a stretched sheet of watercolour paper, gently sketch in the composition with a pencil. Wet the whole surface with the Hake. Stroke the greens of the background into the wet surface, using a round soft nylon brush. Let this layer dry and apply further washes if required.

3 Flat nylon brush Use the flat nylon brush to produce both brushy strokes for the flower head and scuffs of texture on the butterfly wings. For juicy strokes, the brush should be loaded generously, but for scuffing it should be sparsely loaded. Keep a spare sheet of paper to hand on which you can remove excess paint before applying the scuffs.

4 Rigger brush & round soft brush Use a couple of Riggers to redraw and add line-work where necessary, with light and dark colour mixes. Dark colours create linear accents, which are very useful at this stage. Finish off with lights and highlights, which can be painted up to the line-work. To reduce any line-work that has become too dominant, simply paint over it, using some of the light colours.

The delicate nature of a white butterfly alighting on a lavender flower head provides the perfect subject with which to practice various brushes and different techniques. Each brush brings its own unique quality, from the gentle strokes of the soft round brush, to the juicy strokes of the stiff nylon.

Once the dark underpainting and line drawing has been completed, the lighter colours are applied mainly wet-on-dry.

Strokes within the flower head are restricted to the use of a stiff nylon brush, which produces textured lights and highlights.

The wings are painted with the round soft nylon brush, which contains and controls the dark scuffs laid earlier. As the colours move toward white at the wing edges, a second round soft nylon is kept close at hand. This is brought into action to soften some of the paint edges, while still wet, to achieve gentler gradations between the values. This can be seen along the top of the wing folds, which softly catch light from above.

Final details, both light and dark, are judiciously applied with the Rigger.

Why do I need a palette?

As in painting with oils or watercolours, the acrylic painter needs an area on which to mix paint, particularly one that allows for control of those mixes. Of equal importance is the need for temporary storage of paint squeezed from the tube during any painting session. The ideal palette therefore is one that offers a surface on which to mix colours, along with areas in which to deposit the required paints.

HOWEVER, ACRYLIC PAINTS and mediums are somewhat different to watercolours and oils. Although they dry swiftly, like watercolours, the resemblance ends there, for once dried, acrylic paints cannot be re-dissolved. On the other hand, they are similar to oils, in that they dry with a tough insoluble surface. Oils, however, take time to dry and remain malleable until they do so, unlike acrylics.

The moment acrylic paint leaves its tube or container, the water within the paint begins to evaporate.

Should a thin layer of acrylic paint be applied to a traditional palette, it has the potential to dry within minutes, leaving a solid film of acrylic.

Traditional dry palettes are only suitable for use with acrylic paints and mediums if the surface of the palette is non-absorbent. Otherwise, an absorbent surface, such as wood, will absorb moisture from the paint, speeding up the process of drying. Once dry, the acrylic paint would have an even greater grip on the surface and will simply not come off.

There are times when a standard palette is more practical when painting in acrylics and it is essential therefore to ensure the correct version is chosen to cope with the demands of this fast-drying medium.

Whilst an old ceramic plate may be the choice of some beginners, it will soon become evident that this will prove extremely frustrating. Far better to opt for a palette that offers a large mixing area, plus wells in which to store paint that has been squeezed from the tube.

Although dry plastic palettes are suitable for watercolours, they cannot cope with the demands of painting in acrylics. For once dry, acrylic paint grips tightly onto the plastic surface and is impossible to remove.

When choosing a non-absorbent dry palette therefore, its surface is of paramount importance. It must be so smooth as to allow dried acrylic paint to be scraped cleanly away, with no possibility of any residual particles of dried acrylic paint being left behind. Any particles remaining on the surface would adulterate freshly deposited paint.

A GOOD PALETTE IS MADE FOR THE JOB.
Ideally, any palette used for acrylic painting must be capable of slowing down the drying time of acrylic paints and acrylic colour mixes. Consequently a unique palette has been developed for this purpose, referred to as the stay-wet palette.

Stay-wet palettes not only keep acrylic colours wet during mixing and brush loading, but also protect the temporary cache of squeezed out paint. To achieve this, the palette is centred on a wet atmosphere, in which a constant amount of water is maintained, to compensate for any lost in the paint by evaporation.

The mixing area of this unique acrylic palette comprises several wet layers, the top sheets of which are disposable. As the top layers become soiled and unusable these sheets are constantly changed.

The lower, water-storage section features a layer of sponge or other absorbent material, such as blotting paper. Since such materials are usually soft and would absorb the paint, they are separated from the paint mixes and are overlaid by a semi-permeable membrane which allows the water to seep upwards.

The top layer of this semi-permeable membrane is the mixing surface and is kept constantly damp. As such, it needs to be relatively strong to withstand the pressure of mixing whilst in this wet state and not likely to disintegrate.

A variety of stay-wet palettes are available to acrylic painters, but whatever the type, the size of the mixing area should be given due consideration. The larger the mixing area the better, as this will allow for a greater number of mixes to be worked and the less often the disposable top layer will have to be changed.

By using a stay-wet palette, it is possible to keep paint mixes on the surface for some considerable time. The added feature of a lid would be helpful, as this enables mixes to be stored overnight if required.

Since all successful colour mixing demands the ready supply of generous amounts of paint, it must be taken from the tube and stored in temporary containers in sizeable amounts. The mixing area of a stay-wet palette should not be used for this purpose, for a number of reasons.

First, the area should be maximised to achieve the greater number of mixes. Second, over time, generous paint deposits on the top semi-permeable layers are likely to absorb too much water from beneath and begin to run out of control on the surface. Third, paint deposited on the mixing area will be wasted when the time comes to change the top layers.

Small, but deep, storage pots, with lids, will not only preserve the necessary damp atmosphere between use, but also keep the paint safe during transport.

TIP:
More brushes are lost to acrylic paint drying solid in their hairs than in any other medium. When carried away in the moment of painting, it is all too easy to forget that brushes used with acrylics must be kept constantly wet when in use.

The simple temporary solution is to lay the brush heads down on the wet surface of a stay-wet palette.

Understanding palettes

Some dry palettes are suitable for use with acrylic paints. i.e. Glass or ceramic. NOT WOOD OR PLASTIC.

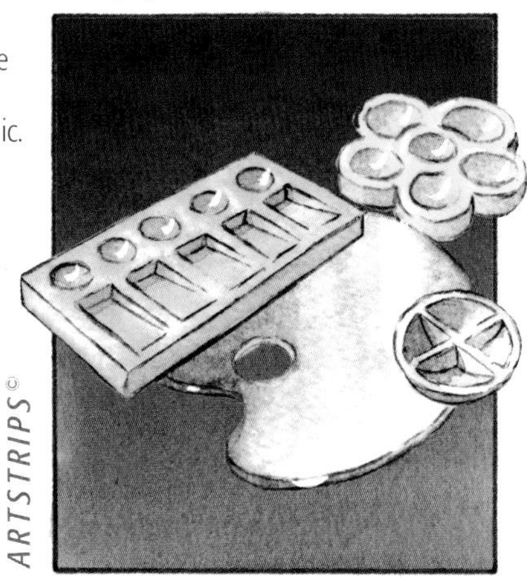

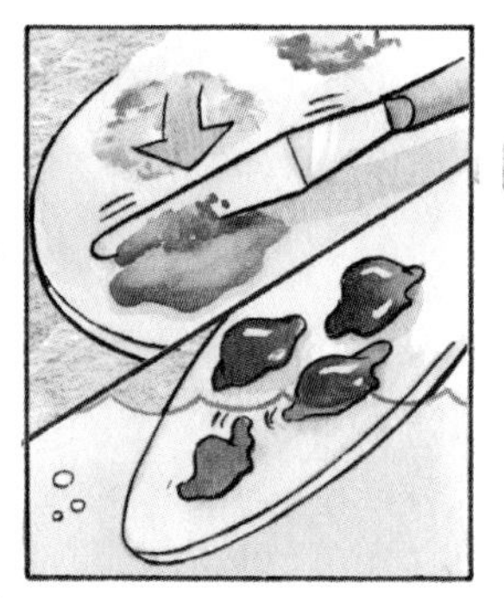

The material of which they are made must allow for paint to be scraped away without damaging their surface - or enable paint to be soaked off.

STAY-WET PALETTE
Specifically designed for acrylics. Features membrane that draws up moisture from underlying water-retaining layer, to keep paint wet.

Make your own stay-wet palette. Get two flat plastic trays. Cut two sheets of blotting paper and two sheets of greaseproof paper to size.

Line tray with 2 layers of blotting paper, followed by two layers of greaseproof. Soak each sheet with water as it is laid in place.

Pour off excess water and with your fingers gently smooth out the top layer of greaseproof paper to remove air bubbles.

Use remaining tray as lid. Invert over first and secure with elastic band. This contained damp environment helps to protect acrylic paints stored overnight.

Acrylic paint sticks to almost any surface, which is of tremendous benefit when it comes to selecting the painting surface. On the other hand, this very characteristic proves somewhat of a dilemma in the matter of choosing an appropriate palette.

There are two deciding factors that will affect your choice. One, opt for a palette that enables you to easily clean off dry acrylic paint, or two, choose one that prevents the paint from drying in the first place.

TIP:
Start-up colours
Start with warm and cool primary colours plus white and black. Arrange in order of their position on the colour circle.

WORKING PAINT STORAGE
Acrylic paint placed in deep storage wells generates an enclosed damp atmosphere. This slows down drying out of paint.

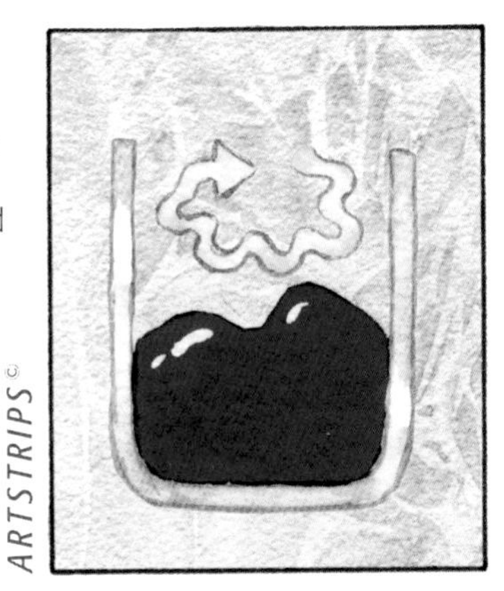

It is essential to keep paint moist. Frequent top-ups with small amounts of water will replace fluid lost through evaporation.

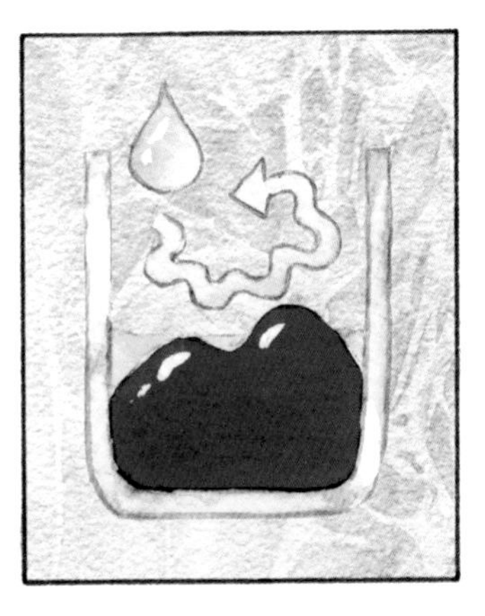

Loaded brush touching sides or bottom of wells will taint acrylic paint within them. Ensure deep quantity of paint to prevent this happening.

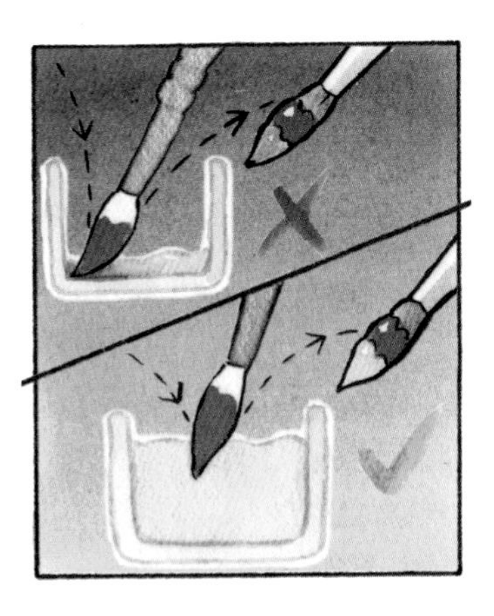

Most stay-wet palettes feature storage wells with lids. Ideal for long periods of storage and/or transport. Small jam jars make perfect alternatives.

The question is this. Why would anyone wish to allow acrylic paint to dry out on the palette and therefore, what is the point of a dry palette? Although seemingly a waste of paint, there are instances where choosing to use a dry palette makes practical sense. Dry palettes are much easier to handle when working out of doors, since they are simple to hold in the hand like a watercolour or oil painting palette. Paint is allowed to build up on the surface until the end of the painting session and then is either scraped and chipped off, or soaked away.

Stay-wet palettes work on the principle of keeping the mixing surface wet to prevent the acrylic paint from drying out. This requires that they should ideally be kept level, to prevent any water from draining away from the various layers. Keeping a stay-wet palette level, while being held in the hand during a painting session, is strenuous. More often than not, it is therefore placed on an adjoining table.

However, stay-wet palettes do keep the paint fluid and workable for much longer than a dry palette. Furthermore, it is possible to save mixes for the following day's painting session.

One solution is to have a dry palette for working out and about, with a stay-wet palette specifically for painting indoors.

Palettes in practice

THE CREATION OF effective paint mixes not only requires a good palette, it also requires an understanding of how to control the consistency of the mixes. In turn, the ability to achieve various paint consistencies enables the acrylic painter to fully appreciate how layering is maximised within a painting to successfully build colour.

By practising these simple exercises on watercolour paper, you will become familiar with a variety of techniques that will prove invaluable in extending your repertoire. Do not worry about colour accuracy; instead, concentrate on the consistency of the palette mixes and how the various brushes are used to achieve the different techniques. These four practice sketches were painted using mixes of coloured greys, in which colours were dulled with the addition of their complementaries. White was also used in the mixes.

Wet on wet palette mix

The consistency of the palette mix for this wet-on-wet sketch needs to be kept stiff. This is done by keeping the paint mix as deep as possible on the palette, so that it does not become over-diluted by the wet surface of the palette. A Hake brush is used solely for the purpose of wetting the paper surface. The soft round brush will load well with paint and is then easily shaped with the thick paint into a chisel shape. Exploit this shape to produce a variety of differing strokes across the wet surface, from thick strokes to thin line.

Wet on dry palette mix

The consistency of the palette mix for this wet-on-dry sketch needs to be kept to washes of colour. This is done by thinly spreading the paint across the palette, so that it absorbs more water from the wet surface of the palette and becomes quite fluid. If required, a little more water and medium can be added. Thin washes or strokes of paint are applied with a medium size, round soft brush.

A second round brush is kept at hand for losing any harsh edges of some of the brush-strokes, wherever necessary. This requires wetting the edge of a still-wet paint stroke, so that it runs into the newly wetted area. The mix for wetting is made up of equal quantities of water and gloss medium, which can be stored in a pool on the palette.

Dry brush palette mix

The consistency of the palette mix for this dry brush sketch needs to be kept as stiff as possible. This is done by keeping the paint mix as deep as possible on the palette and, if necessary, by gently drying the palette surface with an absorbent tissue, before transferring any paint to it. Do not fully mix the colours - instead, allow the mix to remain streaky. Applied to the surface, streaky mixes will be more visually exciting when brush-strokes are composed of more than one colour. This also helps to demonstrate the colours of which the grey mixes are composed.

To reduce loading of colour mix in the brush, pull it across the palette surface, away from the deep paint mix. A sparsely loaded brush will more readily produce scuffs and scumbles.

In some areas, allow the brush to pick up more paint and, in this instance, daub the colour on the painting surface, rather than drag it.

NOTE

WET ALL BRUSHES BEFORE USE, BUT SQUEEZE OUT EXCESS MOISTURE ON AN ABSORBENT TISSUE.

Fluid line palette mix

Once again, the paint is turned into fluid washes with the addition of a generous mix of water containing a little medium. Although the Rigger brush is to be used to produce the line, it is too fragile for mixing paint on the palette. This should be done with a larger round soft brush.

First, load the Rigger generously, by taking paint from the centre of the fluid pool. Then, load it sparingly, by pulling the paint across the palette, away from the pool. By changing the method of loading the same Rigger, you will be able to achieve a multitude of variable strokes without resorting to other brushes. Some brush-strokes will be broad and fluid, others dragged into linear scuffs.

Exercise for palettes

WET ON WET PALETTE MIX Begin the succulent leaves using wet-on-wet brush-strokes. For the greens of the leaves the wet-on-wet palette mix is fluid, rather than stiff, with water added to the colour mix of [Yo+Bg+ro+TW]. The paper surface is wetted overall with the Hake brush before applying the green for the leaves. Once all the leaves have been completed move on to the pot. This fluid mix of [Bp+Yo+ro+TW] has even more water added to it. Before applying to the paper surface, wet only the area of pot, using a large round soft brush.

DRY BRUSH PALETTE MIX The heavy texture of the plant stem is achieved with a series of scuffs. Transfer a generous amount of texture/modelling paste to the palette and then add it to a dry mix of [Ro+Yo+bp+TW] with no added water. The round brush shapes well in this mix and the flattened end is used to scuff colour down the stem. Linear strokes are achieved by using the edge of the flattened end.

WET ON DRY PALETTE MIX A fluid mix of [Yo+Bg+ro+TW] is made fluid for the wet-on-dry strokes, applied with a medium round soft brush, to further describe the leaves. A second brush can be used quite aggressively to soften edges of still-wet paint, with the knowledge that underlying acrylic colours will not lift. This brush is loaded with a fluid mix of water and medium, pre-mixed on the palette surface.

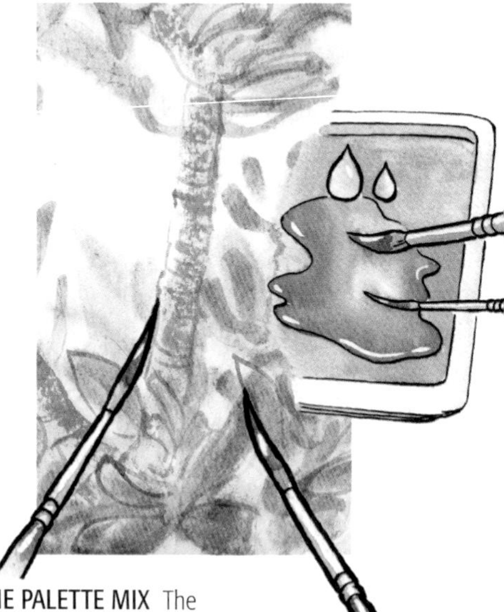

FLUID LINE PALETTE MIX The final mix for the linework is the most fluid of them all. In this instance generous amounts of water and a little extra medium are added to the mix on the palette. Since the Rigger brush is too fragile for mixing the colours, use a round brush to do this. Consolidate the structure of the study using line-work applied with the Rigger.

What at first may appear to be a complex subject can be rendered much simpler by the use of fluid, directional brush-strokes. Various palette mix consistencies and brushes are brought together to maximise the various techniques with which you can effectively achieve this study.

The starting point is a piece of stretched watercolour paper. Use a loose, scribbly drawing to initially describe the rhythms of the leaves, rather than concentrating on any detail.

Continue with wet-on-wet and restricted wet-into-wet to establish layers of soft focus. Follow these with wet-on-dry strokes and scuffs to begin the process of rendering sharper details. Be judicious in the use of sharp detail, since the intention is to achieve a simple, suggestive study, offered by the underlying softer strokes.

As you move into the final line-work with the Rigger, keep it to a minimum. Use the line to proper effect, to define confusing areas of softer strokes, or to bring certain elements forward, where appropriate, so they appear in front of others.

What surface do I need for painting in acrylics?

The answer is simple. Acrylic paint is uniquely different to other media, for it can be painted onto almost any material.

It is one of the most versatile and strongest of all painting mediums and is also flexible. These attributes result from the medium (glue) that fixes the pigment to the surface, which is a form of plastic; hence the term acrylic paints.

WHATEVER THE SURFACE, be it smooth or textured, natural or artificial, it is more than likely acrylic paint will adhere to it. As to whether or not the surface requires priming, there is no easy answer, as it entirely depends on what role the surface finish will play in the completed painting. Whatever the finish, it will react to the paint and this needs to be taken into account.

On absorbent materials such as paper, card, wood, canvas, plaster and stone, the paint will, when first applied, sink into their surfaces like a stain. The impact of its colour and value will merge into that of the base material. On the other hand, non-absorbent surfaces of materials such as slate, metal and glass, may at first repel the paint.

If these qualities do not suit a particular technique or effect, the surface will need to be prepared and in acrylic painting this could not be simpler.

PREPARING ABSORBENT SURFACES

Were you working in oils, the base surface would require sizing and then priming. Sizing is the method used to fill in all holes, scratches etc in a surface to render it less absorbent. Priming is a coating that makes the surface less likely to absorb the paint medium and also provides added tooth.

In acrylic painting these two processes occur as one, simply referred to as priming. When a coat of acrylic paint or medium is applied to any surface it not only fills in the holes, but also dries hard as an overall plastic film, or skin on the surface. This skin is itself non-absorbent.

NOTE

CHECK TO ENSURE CANVAS BOARDS OR CANVASSES HAVE BEEN PRIMED FOR USE WITH ACRYLIC PAINTS, AS NOT ALL ARE SUITABLE FOR THIS WATER-BASED MEDIUM.

There are many options for priming, the choices being entirely personal to the individual painter and his, or her, particular techniques.

One of the cheapest methods is to use standard acrylic household emulsion paint, water it down a little and apply several coats. Another is to take PVA or woodworking adhesive, water that down and again, apply several coats. This is possible because the medium in these products is of the same family as the medium in acrylic paint.

For stronger, more professional bonds, turn to acrylic medium, acrylic paint or an acrylic primer, which are specifically produced for the job.

Acrylic primer is pre-mixed for immediate application. It dries opaquely and evenly on the surface and provides a gentle tooth, which is very pleasant to paint on.

One of the most pleasing is acrylic gesso primer, available in either black or white. Gesso is gypsum powder, a form of chalk/fine plaster, which imbues the primer with a unique cushion-like quality that is, nevertheless, very solid and strong.

Gesso primers were used in the past to create satin-smooth, glassy surfaces on which icon painters would produce exquisite masterpieces.

A personal favourite of mine, gesso primers are now available in acrylic form and are equally suitable for paper, card, wood or canvas.

PREPARING NON-ABSORBENT SURFACES

Non-absorbent surfaces often repel acrylic paint because it is water-based. Any grease must therefore be removed from their surfaces.

The acrylic primer, or paint mix itself, can be made more acceptable by reducing surface tension in the water, so that they spread more easily. Simply add a few drops of liquid soap or water-tension breaker to the mix or, wipe the surface with a little of either, before applying the paint.

PREPARING SURFACE TEXTURES

One of the most exciting aspects of acrylic painting is the ease with which you can create textured surfaces, for which a considerable number of specific acrylic texture pastes are available.

Textures can be rendered smoothly or heavily as impasto. They can be arbitrary, moving in different directions to excite overlaid brushwork; or structural, moving across the surface like a mosaic pattern, carrying the eye to suggest structure or movement.

All of which enables the acrylic painter to be adventurous, since the painting surface can become rich and exciting, even before the first brush-strokes of colour are laid.

PRE-PRIMED SURFACES

Although these methods demonstrate how the acrylic painter consequently has access to the widest possible choice of base material and surface textures, off-the-shelf options are also available.

These include primed and textured papers specifically prepared for acrylic painting, acrylic boards, canvas boards, canvasses and so on.

Understanding surfaces

SELF-PRIMING
Absorbent materials such as paper allow the first layer of acrylic to soak in. Once dry however, further layers lie on the surface.

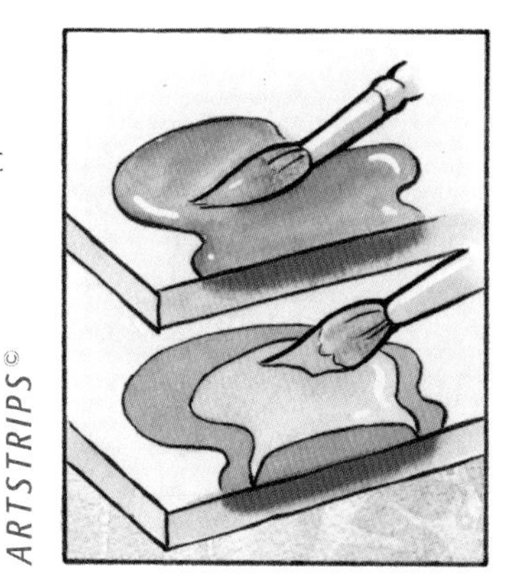

Watercolour papers come in different thicknesses. Also feature inherent textures of various patterns and strengths.

More choices of colours and values are also available in pastel papers and hand-made papers. ENSURE THAT CHOSEN PAPER IS LIGHTFAST.

SUPPLEMENTAL PRIMING
Paper (or card) can be made less absorbent and stronger by priming with acrylic gesso primer. This also imparts a gentle tooth.

PRE-PRIMED
Alternatively, purchase pre-primed pads of paper, suitable for use with acrylic paints. These feature unique textures.

Acrylic can be used as a self-priming medium for almost any base. This offers acrylic painters a tremendous choice of not only what ground to paint on, but also access to a wide choice of surface finishes and textures.

For example, if the ground is an absorbent one, thin fluid washes of acrylic would act like a surface stain, rather than as a wash or stroke of colour. This could be very desirable. Chinese brushwork, admired for its fluidity, is created on very absorbent paper, something that could be exploited as a method of starting off a painting, or as a complete technique.

Once the acrylic dries, it benefits the base in two ways, for it produces a primed and strengthened surface. Fragile bases and surfaces could be therefore rendered more stable, simply by coating them with a painted layer of acrylic. Even powdery surfaces, such as a layer of pastels can be stabilized in this manner, leading to a host of mixed media opportunities.

MATERIALS WITH GRAINS, such as wood, need to be filled with filler (household) or acrylic texture paste if a smooth surface is required. The ground can then be primed…

…with any number of primers i.e. standard acrylic-based household emulsion, acrylic paint, acrylic medium or acrylic primer. Thin gently with water if necessary.

ACRYLIC PRIMED CANVAS is another option. Available in stretched or pad form.

Acrylic texture/modelling paste omprises acrylic medium combined with various strong materials. i.e. marble dust, pumice, glass, ground silica.

Texture paste can be used to create smooth or impasto (textured) surfaces on any suitable ground…

…and can also effect a mosaic of impasto strokes to suggest structure or movement in the subject.

Any created surface will directly affect the finish of the painting. Working with acrylics therefore offers any painter the widest possibilities in this respect.

Should a smooth surface be created, line-work, detail and smooth washes of fluid colour are easily achieved. A textured surface, on the other hand, offers character, structure and movement. It will fracture brush-strokes, readily producing the scuffs and scumbles, the most effective technique for creating visual textures.

Since acrylic medium and acrylic paint dry so quickly, it is a simple matter to create a specific surface before the first stroke of colour is even applied. Acrylic paint itself will also perform its role in creating a unique surface, as it is built up in layers.

What is more, adding mediums to the paint, be they fluid or stiff, offers an extra dimension to the surface and extends your repertoire of techniques.

NOTE

When dry, acrylic surfaces are much more flexible than oils and finished canvasses and can easily be rolled without sustaining damage.

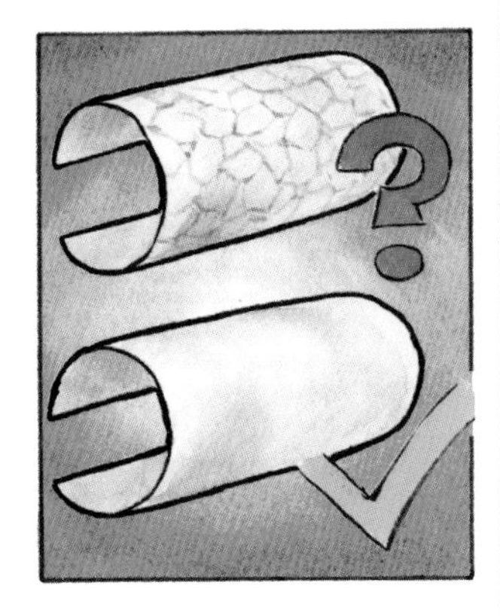

Surfaces in practice

Hot pressed watercolour paper

Pools of fluid paint are laid onto the dry smooth surface of hot pressed watercolour paper, using a large Rigger brush. To prevent the pooling paint from running out of control it is necessary to work flat. As pools of colour touch one another on the paper surface, they will merge and mix.

The smooth surface produces very sharp edges to the areas of wash. A peculiarity of pooling in this manner is that the pigment tends to collect more heavily at the edges of the wetted areas. When dry, this tiny 'wall' of pigment makes the colour edges appear even sharper.

Card

The base material for this sketch is a discarded piece of acid-free mount card, featuring a gently textured surface. The card was primed with a layer of acrylic gesso primer.

The paint is applied a little more thickly than the first study and the brush less generously loaded. This results in scuffed brush marks catching the ridges of the surface over which they are pulled. Both the card texture and the gesso primer thus have an effect on the quality of these strokes. A flat brush, presented at a very close angle to the surface, should be used to facilitate directional scuffed strokes.

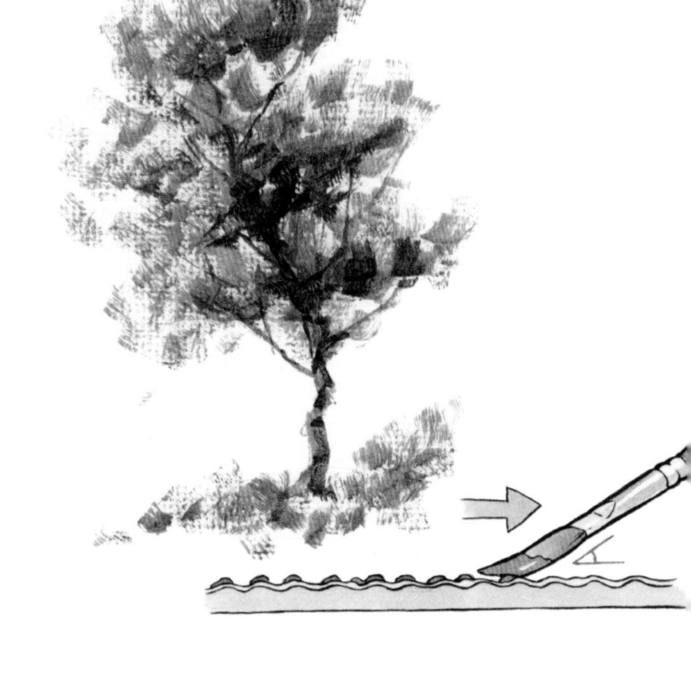

Canvas paper

Whereas canvas paper was used for this study, canvas board or primed canvas will do equally well. Fluid transparent washes, colour mixed with added water and acrylic gloss medium, are brushed directly onto the surface weave. A round soft brush is used to describe the leaf masses and a large Rigger brush to execute the line-work. Colour mixes, being wet, run together as they touch, while their edges, being applied wet-on-dry, remain sharp. The noticeable feature of this surface is the manner in which the washes run into and discover the weave of the surface.

NOTE

ALTHOUGH THIS EXERCISE RELIES SOLELY ON THESE FLUID WASHES OF TRANSPARENT COLOUR MIXES, A FURTHER LAYER OF STIFF PAINT COULD BE USED TO SCUFF THE RIDGES OF THE WEAVE.

Acrylic texture/modelling paste

The surface is not an inherent one, it has been created with acrylic texture/modelling paste, applied over an acid-free card base that was prepared as before. The texture paste is exploited and directional brush-strokes applied to describe the leaf masses, before any colour is painted on. These textured brush-strokes are achieved through the use of a stiff, oil painter's bristle brush.

Leave to dry thoroughly before applying fluid transparent washes of colour. Use a round soft brush for the leaf masses and the Rigger for trunk and branches. This time around, the fluid washes will discover the nooks and crannies in the textured surface of the texture paste, created by the bristle brush.

This study was completed on a piece of discarded, acid-free, mount card, which features a gentle weave texture on its surface. This was prepared by priming the textured surface of the card with a coating of acrylic gesso primer. Although priming is not absolutely necessary, it was used here to render the surface less absorbent and to break up the regular, soft surface pattern and to produce a brushy alternative.

The key to this exercise is the layering process, building from light to dark and back to light again in four paint layers. Start off with a feint, loose, scribbly pencil outline of the composition.

First Paint Layer
Apply fluid washes across the surface with a large Rigger brush. Colour mixes are made very fluid with the addition of water.

Second Paint Layer
Create fluid mixes of transparent colour, with medium now added to the mix. These mixes will be of a more sticky consistency and the surface will react to the brush-strokes in a quite different manner. Keep the washes fluid and use various brushes to describe the leaf masses and apply directional strokes for branches and grasses etc.

Third Paint Layer
This layer comprises of darker, thicker scuffs of colour, applied with a flat nylon brush. Keep these vigorous, drawing the brush in directions that best describe the structure of the subject.

Fourth Paint Layer
Finally, the brightest colours, stiffened with the addition of texture paste, are dripped and dragged onto the surface, thus creating impasto highlights.

Exercise for surfaces

The card's gently textured surface is slightly roughened by applying acrylic gesso primer. When the first fluid washes of colour are applied with a large Rigger brush, the colour tends to run, especially when working upright – this could be exploited. Alternatively, try loading the brush a little less generously to reduce the flow of paint.

Mixing the paint with acrylic medium, rather than water, produces a more viscous mix. This does not run in the same way, even on the upright surface. These first, thinned layers of paint, whether mixed with water or medium, flatten considerably as they dry, leaving only a gently textured surface for the next stage.

Scuffing the stiffer paint on such a mild texture has to be swiftly and gently executed, with the flat brush held at a very low angle to the surface. This ensures the paint is deposited irregularly on the surface, allowing the undercolours to show through and play their part.

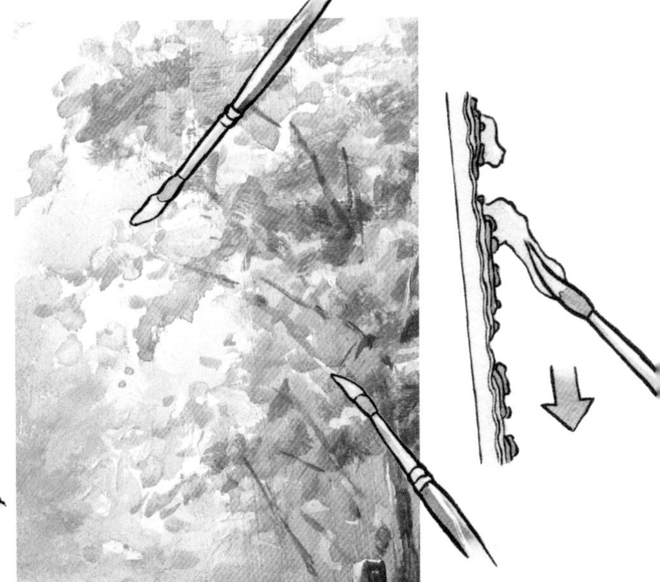

The paint is now stiffened with the addition of texture paste. Return to the Rigger brush and ensure it is heavily loaded. The surface grain of dried paint will now pull the stiff colour from the brush and it is allowed to drip from the brush, leaving a thick textured highlight.

Why is colour mixing so important?

Over the centuries, pigments have been refined in line with availability. Colour ranges have also changed according to the fashion of the day. Although today's artist is blessed with a vast array of colours and qualities of paint, this in itself can prove very confusing, particularly for those new to painting.

CONFUSION FROM THE OUTSET will only lead to frustration, as would lack of knowledge in how colours work and how they can be exploited. This in turn leads to unnecessary mistakes being made in the choice of colours acquired.

The simplest option is to start off with a nucleus palette of colours, which is then expanded as you become more comfortable with mixing colours and develop a particular style in painting. Painters tend to gravitate towards certain subjects and these will also have a bearing on the palette of colours most often used.

Starting off from a firm base of a nucleus palette is particularly important in acrylic painting. From a practical perspective, the paints have to be kept wet while in use. If allowed to dry, acrylic paints simply become unusable. With a limited palette it is far easier to control this, especially when you stop to consider that due care and attention has to also be paid to your brushes and the surface.

Having a limited palette of colours, allows for large amounts of colour to be laid out on the palette during a painting session. A greater number of colours would require a larger palette surface, or limit the amount of colour that could be initially dispensed onto the surface. There is nothing more frustrating than having to constantly replenish supplies of paint during a painting session.

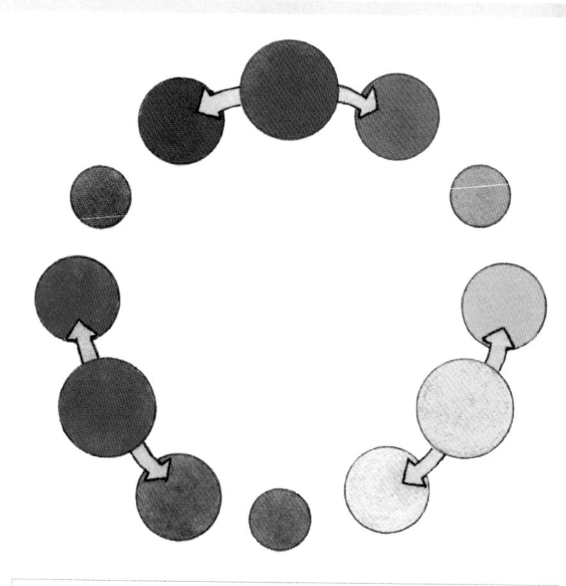

COLOUR REFERENCE

Red-purple	[Rp]
Red-orange	[Ro]
Blue-purple	[Bp]
Blue-green	[Bg]
Yellow-orange	[Yo]
Yellow-green	[Yg]
Titanium White	[TW]

COLOUR MIXING

Where the pre-fix letter is shown in capitals this denotes a larger quantity of that particular colour.

Conversely, where the pre-fix letter is shown in a lower case, this denotes a smaller quantity of that particular colour.

Example:
Bp = **large** amount of blue-purple
bp = **small** amount of blue-purple

The basic theory of colour mixing is quite simple and once acquired is soon expanded through practical experience. Armed with this knowledge you will be surprised just how enjoyable colour mixing is and how fulfilling, quite apart from the fact that it will make a considerable difference to the way you see the world around you.

Suddenly grey clouds will reveal themselves as not being grey at all, but composed of constantly changing colours. Sunlight will become a fascination and you will want to capture its very essence in your paintings.

Furthermore, colour mixing is not merely about mixing specific colours, it is also about balancing the colours across the composition. It is about exploiting accents and highlights, values and tones, contrasts and subtle values.

Imagine a yellow flower. How can it be made to glow on the surface? What colours and values need to be placed behind it to make the flower really outstanding?

Once you acquire the secrets of colour mixing, this becomes second nature and all the time you spend on practising and experimenting with colours will pay off handsomely.

SETTING OUT A PALETTE

Apart from the theory of colour mixing, there are practical aspects to consider. How should you lay out the palette, how are mixes made on its surface and what effects do the various painting mediums have on the colours?

The following pages deal with laying out your palette. Work through it slowly, do not expect to take everything in at one go. Colour mixing will be a part of your everyday painting life and you should give yourself time to consider the role it is to play and how you are going to use it.

One of the first things that will strike you is the fact that colours are not referred to by name, but by their colour bias. This is critical in ensuring that a colour mix is not skewed by a colour name that belies the actual nature of the colour.

More importance needs to be placed on the hue of the colour and where it lies on the colour circle. To know this, is to know its properties, what to expect from the colour and with which colour it could be replaced, if the original choice is unavailable.

Acrylic paints are the most versatile, for they can be rendered either transparently or opaquely, even within one painting. Thus, not only can colours be mixed on the palette, they can also be layered, in effect mixed, on the surface.

TIP:

Although every effort is made in the printing of books to achieve colour accuracy, it is far better not to judge your own results against those in the tutorials. Even in a room full of painters working on the same subject, the results of individual colour mixing would vary slightly. Variations do not denote failure, just as results differing from the tutorials followed in this book should not be seen as mistakes.

PRIMARY COLOURS cannot be achieved through mixing. Instead are used in mixes to achieve other colours.

In theory – primary colours are mixed to create secondary colours.

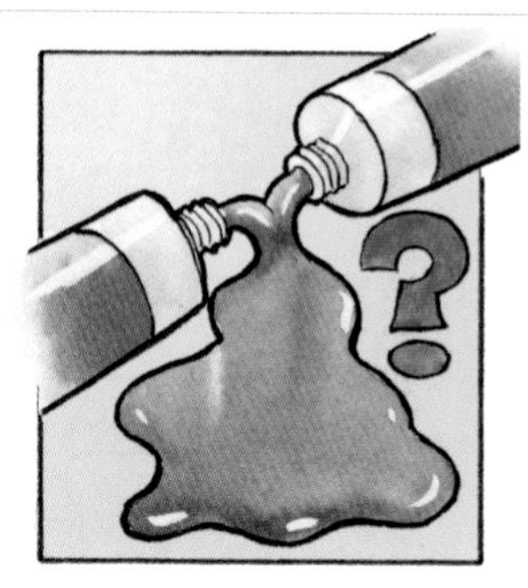

Sometimes this just does not seem to work, because...

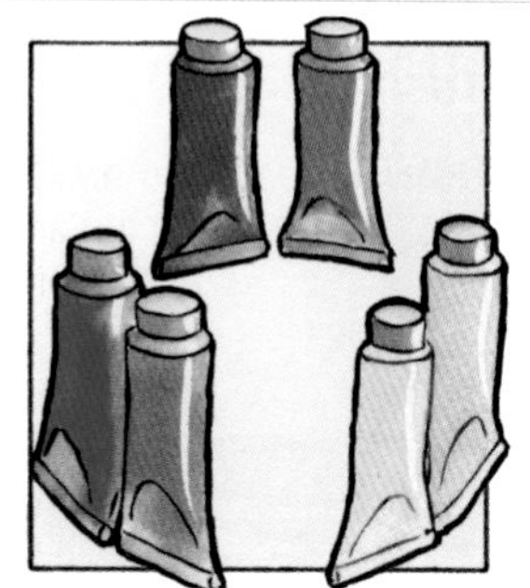

...more than one set of primaries are required. Ones that are biased to the secondary colours they mix best. These six colours form the basic acrylic range.

When depositing quantities in temporary storage containers for palette mixing, it is important to place colours in their colour circle order.

Mixing primaries that are close produces bright secondary colours.

Mixing primaries that are further apart produces dull secondary colours.

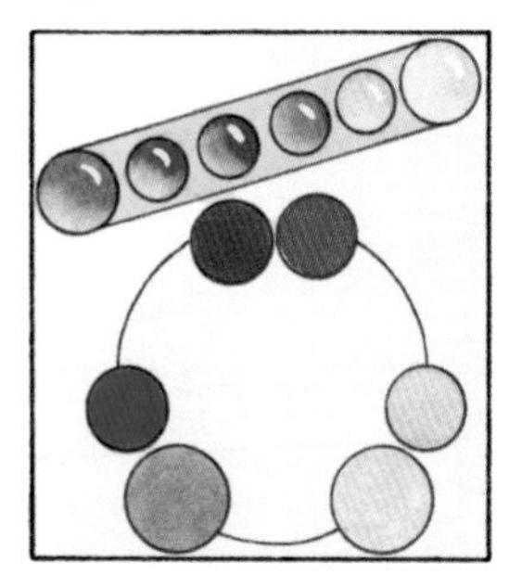

The colours positioned at each end should be considered as close – since this is how they lie on the colour circle.

White can be added to the end of the line. White is used to create opaque tints.

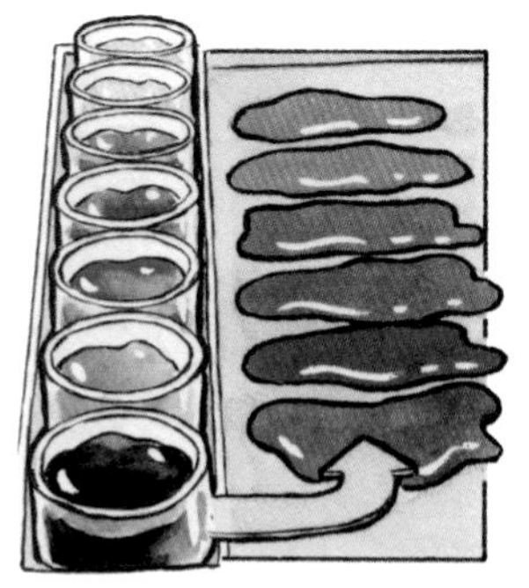

If you want to add black, to create shades, place this at the other end.

Strength of colour mixture is controlled by adding just a little of the strong colour to the edge of the weaker mix. Use the same method...

...when creating transparent mixes, with medium. Always add colour and/or water at the edge of a pool of medium/mix.

Palette mixing

BRIGHT SECONDARY MIXES

Mixing primaries next to one another on the colour circle creates intense (bright) secondary mixes. Red-orange [Ro] +Yellow-orange [Yo] make a good orange, both having an orange bias. The purple grapes are mixed from Red-purple [Rp] + Blue-purple [Bp]. The green of the apples, while both being mixed from Blue-green [Bg] + Yellow-green [Yg] appear to be different. This simple change is made by adding more yellow to the fruit in the foreground and more blue to the one behind.

DULL SECONDARY MIXES

These mixes are created by using primaries at the furthest distance from each other, with a bias away from the secondary colour for which they have been chosen to mix. The orange is therefore mixed from Yellow-green [Yg] + Red-purple [Rp]. The grapes are Red-orange [Ro] + Blue-green [Bg], while the apples are a mix of Blue-purple [Bp] + Yellow-orange [Yo]. Again, the apples have either more yellow (front) or more blue (back) in their mix. Note how grey the grapes have become and while the orange is probably the brightest of the mixes, compare it with the bright orange of close primaries in the first example.

Exercise

BRIGHT SECONDARY MIXES

The bottom half of this exercise is painted in all the bright secondary mixes. In the mixes shown, the first colour is the dominant colour in the final mix. In the diagram the differing sizes of the circles roughly indicate the quantity of each pigment. Examine the mixes of yellow and blue for greens and you will note that the blue is used in smaller quantities. The blue has a more dominant tinting strength; therefore less is required in the mix. Note how adding white to the green (right hand side), dulls the mix, despite these being bright secondaries.

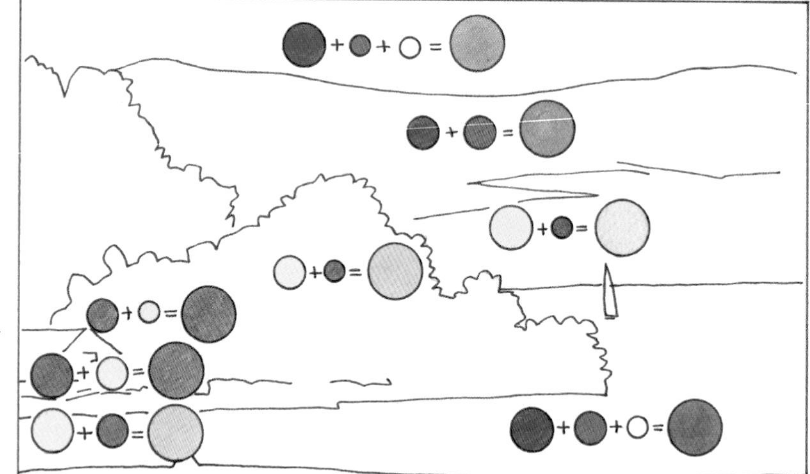

DULL SECONDARY MIXES

The top half of the exercise is painted using dull secondary mixes. Compare the three yellow greens on the distant shore and the trees on the left. The more distant yellow green has been thinned with the addition of a greater quantity of water, than those in front. Try a similar mix, but add white instead of water. It will become immediately obvious that the watered down mix allows the colour to retain some of its intensity, while that containing white, is not only lightened, but is also dulled down.

NOTE

WHITE ALWAYS DULLS COLOURS AND IN SOME INSTANCES THIS MAY BE REQUIRED. BE CAREFUL WITH HIGHLIGHTS HOWEVER, FOR THEY NEED TO BE BRIGHT.

The purpose of this simple exercise is to practice mixing colours on the palette, not to produce an accurate painting. It is painted mainly wet-on-wet, so that the resultant landscape is suggested, rather than rendered in detail. However, final touches of wet-on-dry have been applied to bring focus to relevant areas and are made in the same colour as those directly beneath.

Concentrate on the colours and the mixes; you will learn much about controlling the mixing of secondary colours and what they can do for your painting.

All of the colours are created as secondary mixes. Those on the top half are dull, having been mixed from distant primaries, while the mixes for the bottom half are bright, created from close primaries.

The dull colours seem a little more distant, in spite of the fact that the values (lights and darks) are very close to those of the foreground. One aspect of aerial perspective (a sense of depth through colour) being that colours become duller as they move into the distance.

REMINDER

ADD COLOUR TO A PALETTE MIX BY INTRODUCING IT FROM THE SIDE, RATHER THAN ADDING TO THE CENTRE. THIS ALLOWS FOR CONTROL OVER EXACTLY HOW MUCH OF EACH IS USED, WITHOUT MIXES GOING AWRY AND BECOMING INCREASINGLY LARGER.

Common problems

PROBLEM

During a painting session it is imperative that colours are immediately to hand and freely accessible. This requires that a quantity of each colour is squeezed from the tube into temporary containers. Although deep-welled containers are best suited for this purpose, it is still likely that some soiling and drying out will occur.

A *The first sign of this problem* is often that a skin has started forming across the top of the paint deposit. This can be picked up by the brush and subsequently transferred to the palette mix. If ignored however, the problem will intensify. The paint begins to harden in deeper layers around the edge, leaving a smaller and smaller opening through which the paint deposit can be accessed. Paint already on the brush is accidentally transferred to this hardening area, either soiling the colour and, or, adding to the ever-drying blockage of paint.

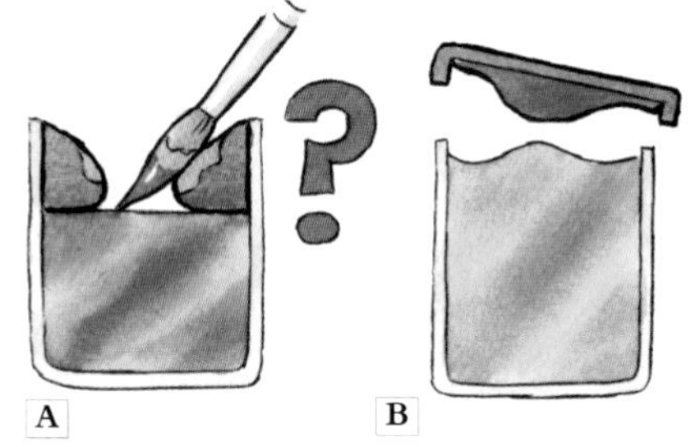

B *In some cases, paint can begin to build up* on the lid and dry there. This becomes thicker with time, lifting more colour from the well and can even prevent the lid from being replaced properly.

SOLUTION

C *Use a blunt knife* to periodically scrape away drying deposits, before they become a problem. Be careful not to let particles of dry paint fall into the wet colour and to eliminate paint around the top, which could prevent the lid from being firmly replaced.

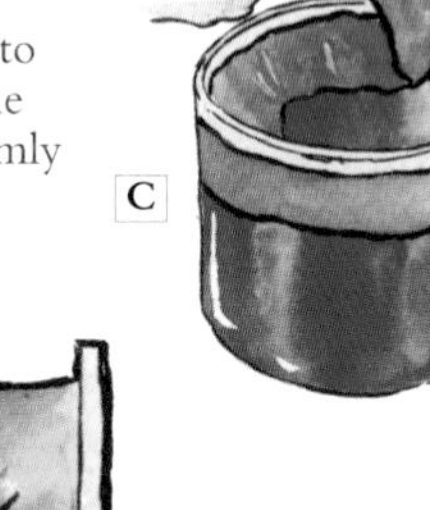

TIP: The few drops of water needed to top up the moisture level in the containers are far better added at the end of a painting session, rather than at the beginning. This will allow the water to seep slowly down into the paint over a period of time, rather than simply being soaked up by the first brush load. Even worse, the uppermost levels of the paint deposit may become too fluid, if the water is not given time to penetrate through.

PREVENTION

D *Often the cause of drying* paint is due to overfilling the paint well in the first instance. Filled to the top, the paint surface is in direct contact with the air.

E *By lowering this level,* a small volume of air is held within the walls of the container. Within this space, the atmosphere becomes damp, as water evaporates from the paint. This damp atmosphere can be topped up with drops of water, so that the paint is less likely to dry out.

F *Do not let* the quantity of paint get too low, or the brush will touch the bottom as you replenish it with colour and is likely to soil the stored paint.

Common problems

PROBLEM

Having mixed a colour on the palette surface, the brush head often bulks up with colour, especially with stiffer mixes. The brush is far too heavily loaded for painting, but a valuable quantity of the colour mix would be lost if the brush were to be wiped on a tissue or cleaned in water. Neither can the excess colour be squeezed out with your fingers. Apart from being messy, the paint is likely to spread to other brushes with disastrous consequences!

The problem cannot be solved by keeping a separate brush for mixing, since the colour it contains is required for painting.

SOLUTION

A Use either a very blunt knife, or an oil painter's knife, to squeeze the excess paint back onto the surface of the palette. Be very gentle, squeezing down toward the point. Use the knife to consolidate any stray colour and wash immediately, before it becomes caked with drying paint. You will find the paint does not hold on to the knife as it does to the brush and the knife easily deposits the paint back on to the palette surface.

B Now the brush can be wiped or squeezed gently and reshaped in a damp or dry absorbent tissue. Ensure that any paint on the ferrule or handle is removed before it dries fast. The brush is now in perfect shape to paint and you can return to the palette to reload the brush head, toward its point. Do not be tempted to wash the brush in water, as this can lead to the paint mix becoming too fluid.

C If there is any danger of the brush beginning to dry toward the ferrule, gently splay the head across the palette during loading. This action will pick up some moisture from the surface of the stay-wet palette. If you do need to add water, merely dip the point of the brush into the water supply and return it to the palette mix.

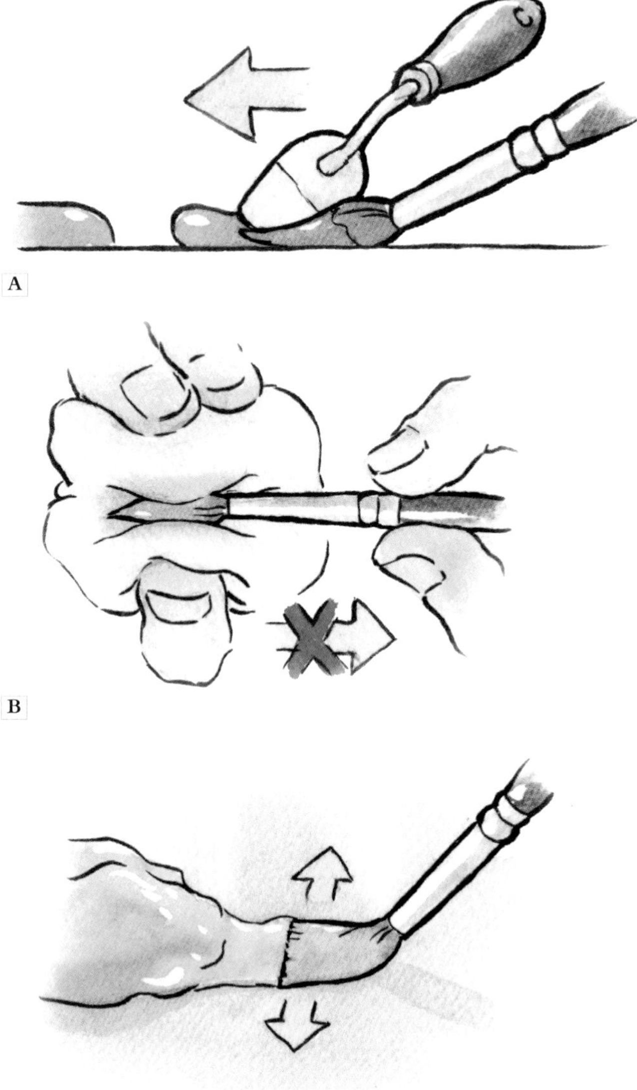

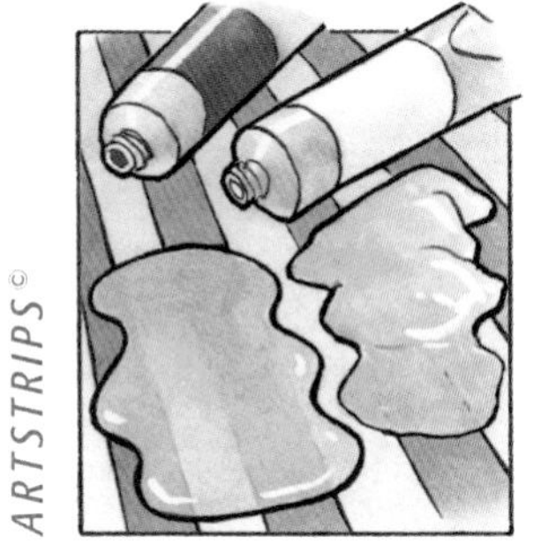

COLOUR TINTS Mixes with added white are known as tints. These can be fluid or stiff.

VISUAL COLOUR MIXING Opaque colours become more transparent as more water and/or medium is added. Dry colour beneath shows through.

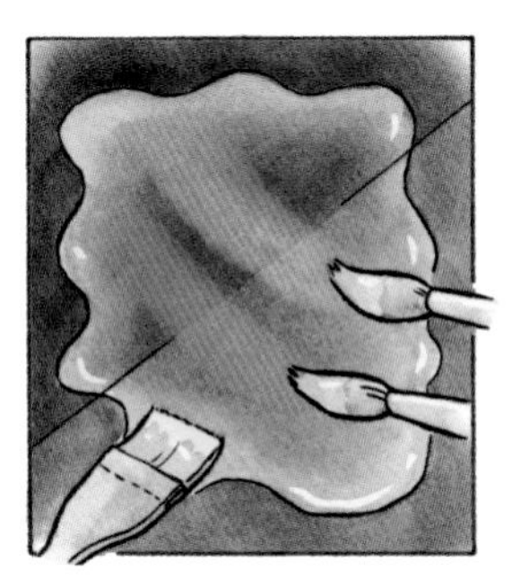

SURFACE COLOUR MIXING Stiffer mixes painted into a wet surface flow and the colours from below show through irregularly.

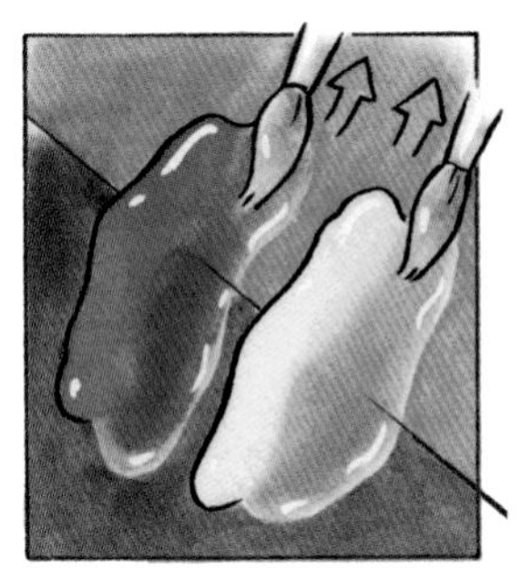

A similar effect occurs when edges are lost.

SCUFFING AND STIPPLING onto a dry surface can be used to achieve both visual texture and colour mix with lower layers.

TEXTURAL COLOUR MIX Use masking fluid applied over white or a colour.

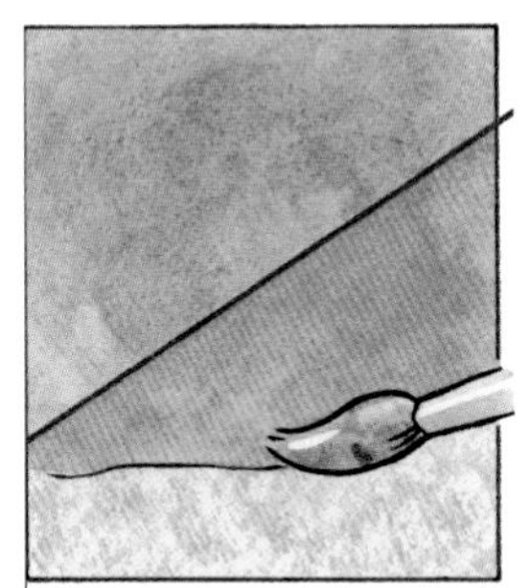

When dry this can be overlaid with a second opaque colour, or semi-opaque wash.

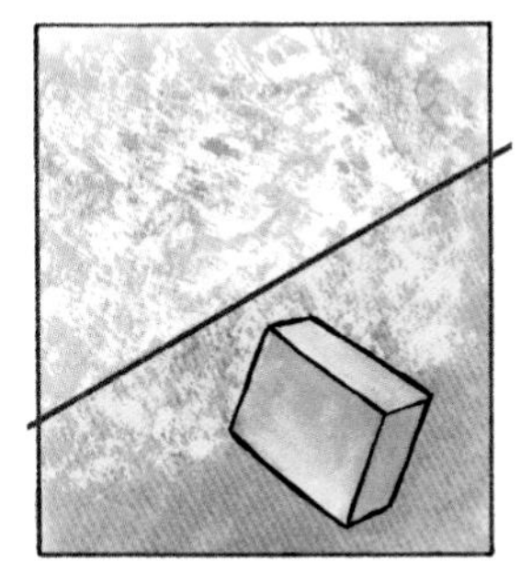

Remove masking fluid once colours are dry to reveal a textural colour mix between the two layers.

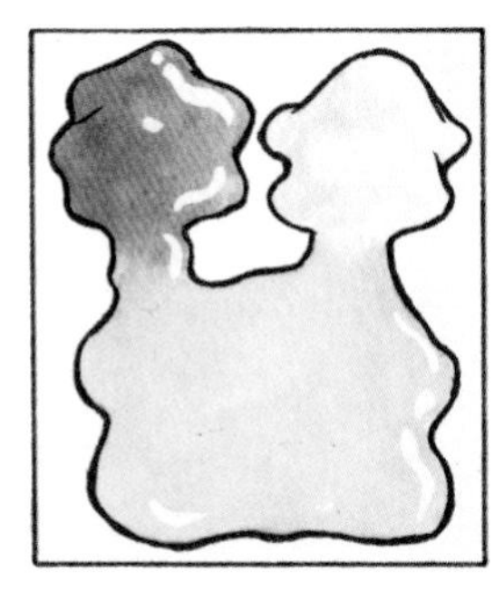

ADDING WHITE to a colour reduces the intensity considerably.

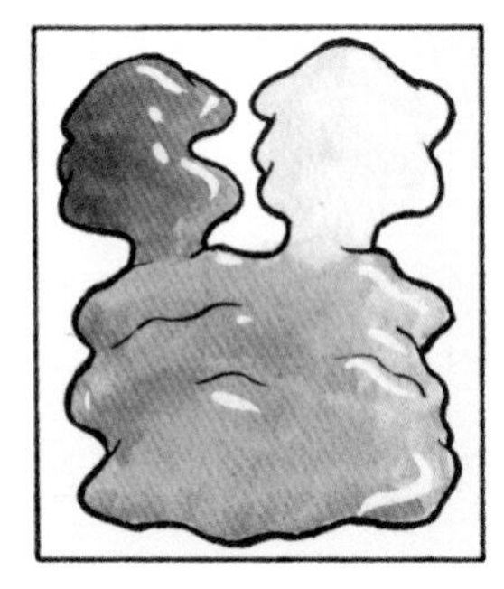

ADDING TEXTURE PASTE to a colour makes it stiffer... but has less effect on strength of colour.

Colour mixes with texture paste are far easier to scumble into and over one another.

INCOMPLETE MIXING ON THE PALETTE produces streaky colour mixes. Far more visually interesting than perfectly mixed paint.

Opaque mixing

These diagrams demonstrate the effect of visual colour mixing between layers, exploited to render the forms of three geometrical shapes. In each case the first layer of colours (top right hand corner) were allowed to dry thoroughly to prevent them physically mixing with the second layer. All mixes had some white added to them, so that they are in effect either opaque or semi-opaque, dependent on the quantity of white and the thickness of the applied layer.

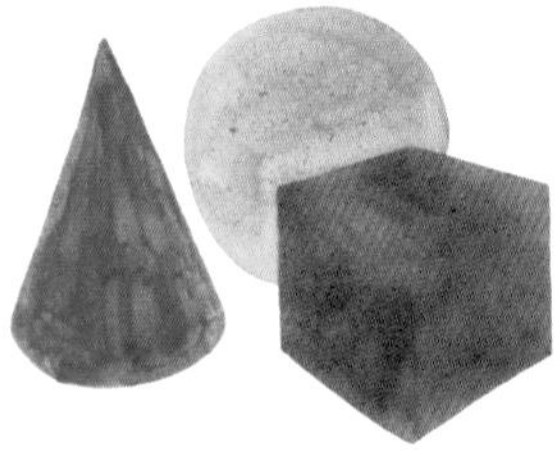

WET-ON-WET : SOFT VISUAL MIXING

Each colour used in the second layer was applied in a graduated wash, in which the fluidity and the amount of white was increased, or decreased, as the wash was applied. Before each section was painted, the specific area was wetted, so that brush-strokes were applied wet-on-wet to soften the effect. The graduated washes were blended to ensure an even finish to the colours. Each form was treated differently, to achieve volume through visual colour mixing. The blue ball has differing values of blue, washed through to light. The green cube has a complementary red overlay and the blue-purple cone is overpainted with various purples and reds, of differing values.

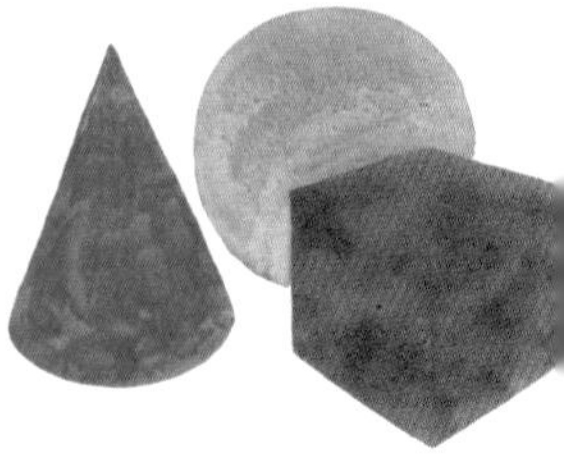

WET-ON-DRY : HARD VISUAL MIXING

In this set the paint was applied wet-on-dry, creating scumbles with exactly the same colour mixes as those used in the wet-on-wet demonstration. The visual colour mixes are now much more textured. The brush-strokes follow the direction of the surface. In the round ball they curve around, while in the box they follow the planes of the various faces. The second layer tended to become duller as white was added. Normally this would be corrected through the application of coloured glazes. Here they were left in their muted form, so that the nature of the tints could be more easily seen.

Exercise

WHITE : PAPER SURFACE

Masking fluid was applied to areas that were to remain as pure white highlights, to protect them from overlaid soft wet-in-wet washes of paint. This naturally created areas that feature sharp edges, which is perfect for the hard planes of the gemstones.

Applied as a solid thin layer for some of the smooth mirror-like surfaces (top), the masking fluid was scuffed elsewhere, to create more broken texture (bottom). The point and tip of the brush is best to apply controlled sharp edges; scuffs being applied with the shoulder of the brush head, dragged across the paper texture.

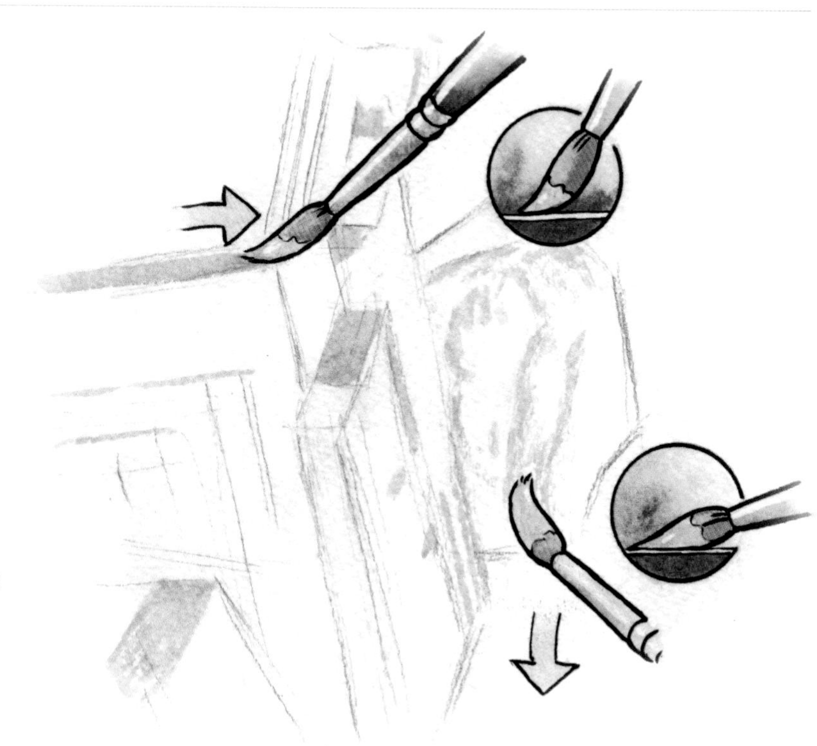

WHITE : OPAQUE PAINT

Reflected softer whites from the gemstone were created by overlaying opaque blue greys and whites, across the dry acrylic soft areas of colours already applied. These strokes are rendered opaque or semi-opaque, dependent on the thickness of the layer and the amount of white in the mix. Where the whites do not completely cover, the colour from beneath shows through, adding to the final colour mix.

Strokes were directional, following the lie of each surface. In some cases, several layers were overpainted to reach the required value, since these lights inevitably fade as they dry.

Some of the masked textured areas were over-scuffed with blue or green grey whites to soften their impact. Note the angle of the brush to the surface – for broad strokes (top) or line-work (bottom).

There are two ways in which white is achieved. One is to utilise the paper surface and this necessitates the use of masking fluid. The second is to apply opaque white paint. Both forms are incorporated into this demonstration. Rocks and stones, particularly gemstones, make excellent subjects for practising colour mixing, since they feature both subtle colour variations and texture. This particular study of Vesuvianite was taken from a photograph, and is particularly engaging because of the contrasts between the translucent surfaces and their reflective qualities.

The inner warm golden browns are kept soft, while the reflected surfaces are mainly cool, light blue greys. The browns suggest depth, while the light blues define the facetted planes of the stone's various surfaces.

The masked white areas and the overpainted blue white highlights in paint are not always separate, but interact and interweave with one another. However, in the final study, it is easy to see the stark difference between the white of the paper and the white created by the pigment.

To the middle right of the stone lies an interesting rounded area of texture. Scuffs have been overpainted with semi-transparent cool washes and with the blue opaque whites, so that all the techniques are interwoven.

Common problems

PROBLEM

Although masking fluid is an invaluable asset to a painter's repertoire of techniques, it can prove exceptionally frustrating unless a few basic working principles are put into practice. However, this does not mean it should be ignored, for this medium is designed to fulfil a quite specific function, which it does exceedingly well. Furthermore it achieves results that could not be obtained in any other way.

MASKING FLUID

Masking fluid is unlike any other medium, in that it is a latex solution, which produces a skin that, in turn, protects the surface to which it has been applied. As such it does not dissolve off the surface, but has to be removed by being gently rubbed away. When properly applied and removed, it has absolutely no adverse effects on the surface or the painting.

Contrary to popular belief it does not destroy brushes, no more so than working with acrylic. As with all working practices, if the care of brushes is maintained there is no reason for them to suffer any damage.

Masking fluid should be considered as one of your paints, albeit a transparent one that renders white highlights. When carefully and thoughtfully applied, as a means of producing sharp-edged detail against the soft qualities of wet-on-wet painting, it cannot be equalled.

Masking fluid is white or very pale in colour, which is difficult to see when dried on the surface. Add a few drops of Indian ink to the main supply and shake well. This will tint the fluid grey.

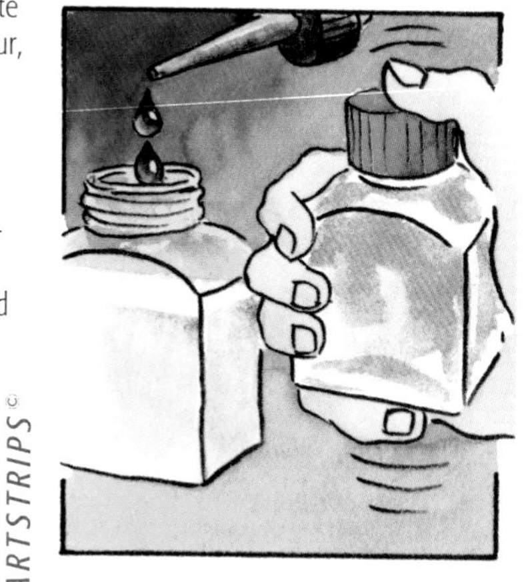

Put a few drops into a section of a ceramic tinting saucer. Never put fresh fluid onto old or drying fluid.

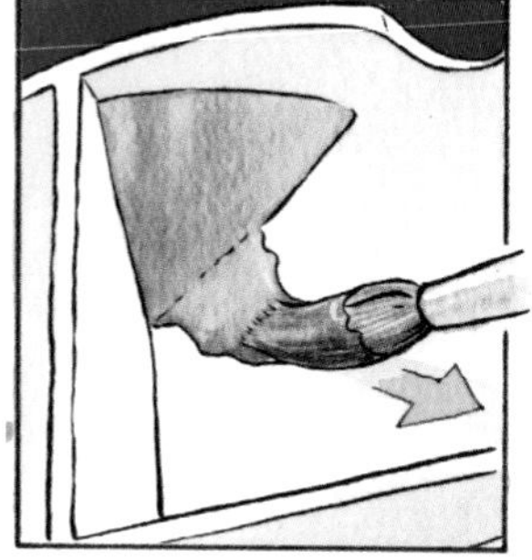

Tip the palette so that the fluid collects in one corner. The brush can now be pulled across the flat area, shaping the brush head as you go.

TIP:
The easiest and gentlest method for removing a dried mask is to gradually rub it away with a kneadable putty rubber.

Avoid pulling the mask away from the surface, as this could result in damage to the surface and/or leave tiny specks of dried latex behind.

A round brush can be flattened to effect more versatile brush-strokes.

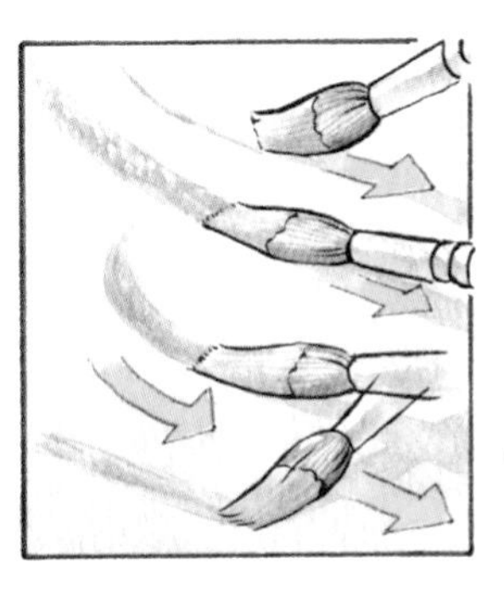

To create a variety of marks, vary direction and pressure of strokes.

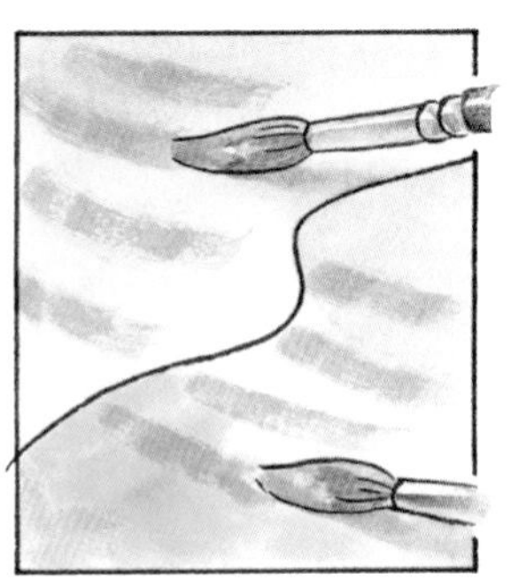

The tinted grey fluid is now easily seen against white paper, or even over light colours.

Tinting the fluid will also help you to avoid applying the mask too heavily (top). Gentle scuffs are often more effective.

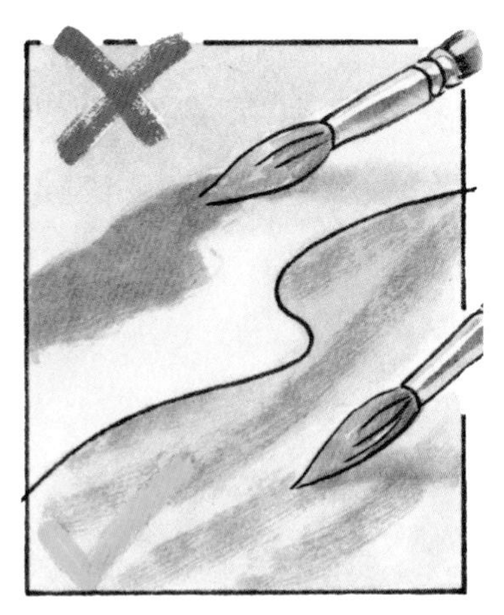

Protect your brush from drying when in use with masking fluid. Create lather on a bar of soap and with your fingernails, gently work it into the base of the brush head.

Wipe away excess soap on a clean absorbent tissue. Leaving soap inside the brush, which will delay drying of the masking fluid in the brush head.

If drying begins, the brush will start to drag on the surface (top). Colour change occurs in the fluid and the brush eventually sticks – stop before this occurs!

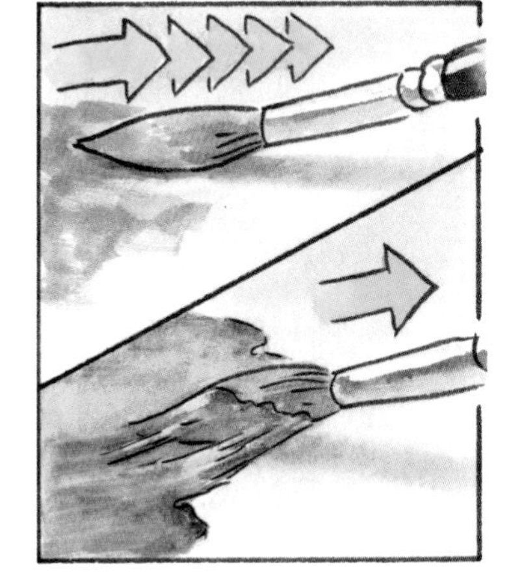

Thoroughly clean brush in water, pushing brush head against the side of the jar to remove mask (top). Use more soap to help remove any remaining masking fluid.

If masking fluid has dried in a brush, do not pull the latex strands, nor tug at the brush hairs, as this will damage the brush. Wash in thinner (turpentine) and then in soap and water as before.

WASHES Mix paint with water (no white). Apply to wet surface. Keep brush in contact with surface at all times to produce an even transparent wash.

SURFACE LAYER MIXING Apply several colour washes, allowing each to dry before overlapping the next. Note the surface mixes that result.

GRADED WASH Apply a continuous wash to a wet surface, but allow colour to run out and gradually ease off brush pressure.

GRADED WASH : LAYERED MIX Allow a graded wash to dry. Invert and paint a second wash, overlapping the first. Lose overlapping edges for gentle gradation.

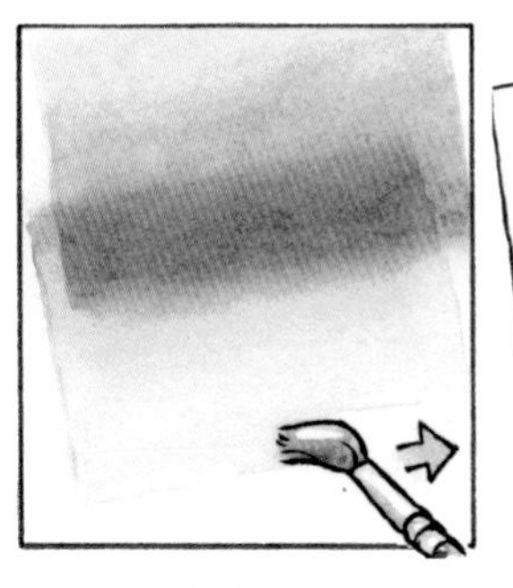

Repeat method but overlap the dark section of the graded washes.

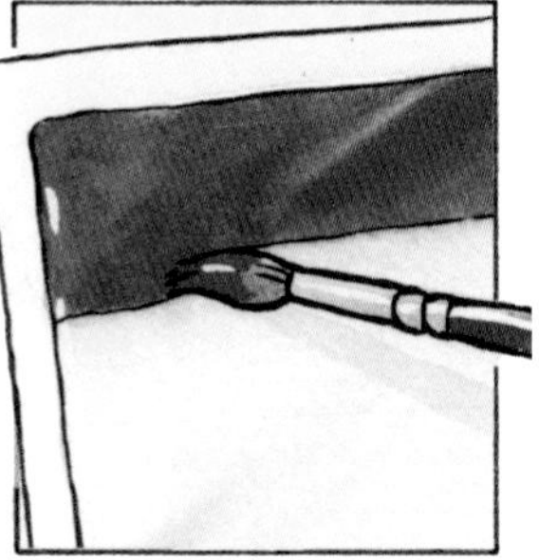

GRADED WASH : COLOUR CHANGE On a wetted surface, start a wash with one colour…

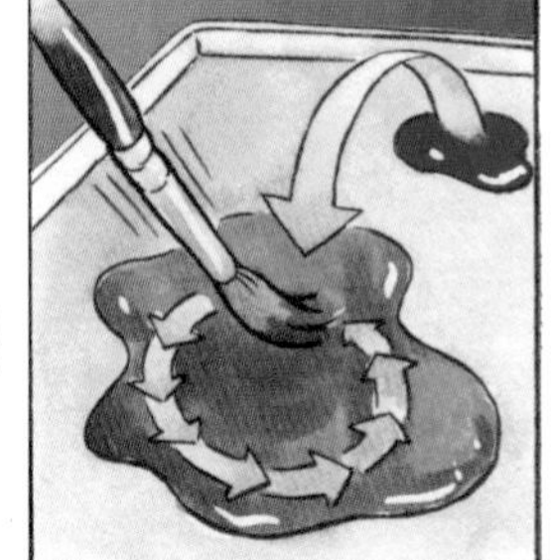

…bring a second colour, little by little, into the generous palette mix and mix well…

… return to applying the wash. Continue to progressively add second colour until colour gradation is satisfactory.

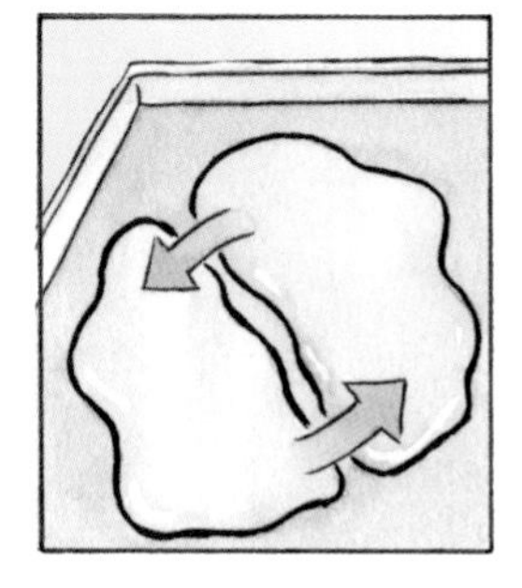

MIXES WITH MEDIUMS Mix a solution of acrylic medium and water across a section of the stay-wet palette.

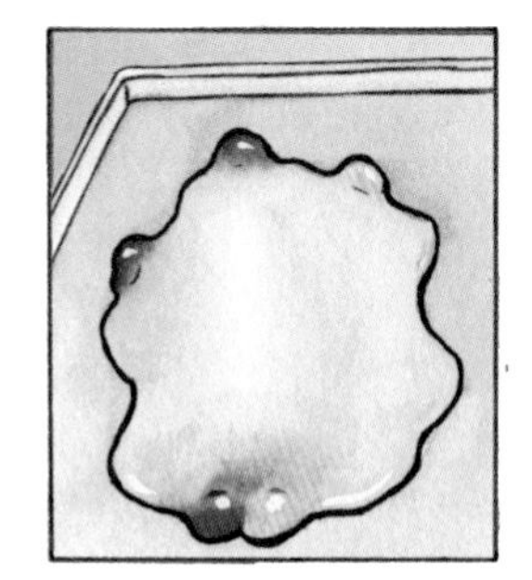

Small amounts of colour are introduced at its edge and mixed together where necessary.

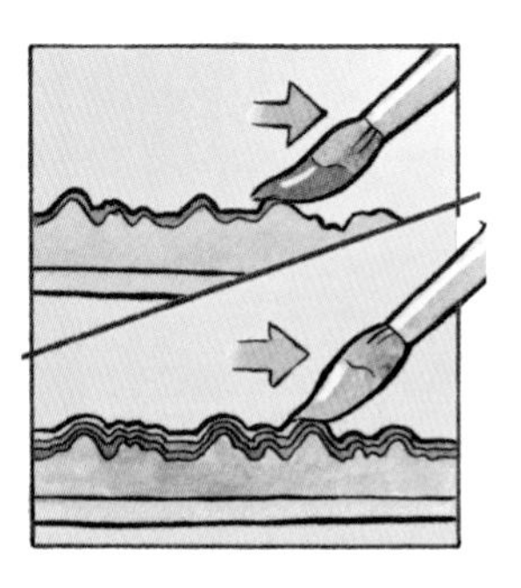

Such mixes of coloured glazes are brushed over impasto surfaces. Several layers of which can be overlaid.

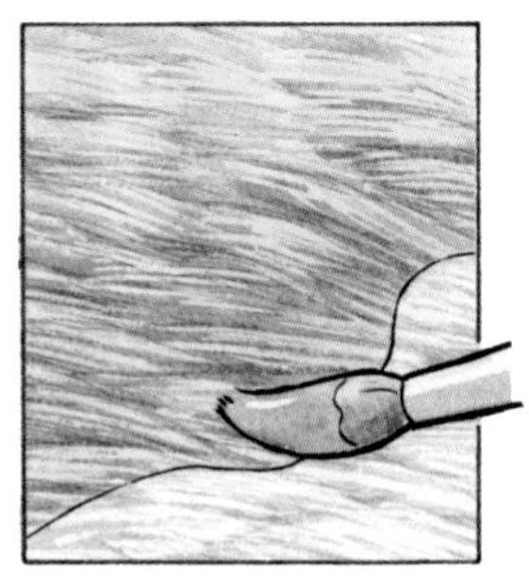

Glazes reveal impasto textures. Glazes also enrich and darken previously laid colours.

Transparent mixing

Two examples of simple graded transparent washes and glazes that have been laid over a gentle pencil outline.

For the first, all colours are mixed with water to create fluid washes. A round soft brush is used to pre-wet each area selectively, so that the relevant wash does not stray. The white of the watercolour paper provides all the white in the colour mixes, since it shows through the thin transparent layer. Each graded wash is produced from one application of the brush, simply easing off the pressure for lighter areas and in some cases, adding a little extra water to the mix. The white highlight line on the surface of the water is created by gently squeezing a clean wet brush in a tissue and running it along the still-wet surface (lift off). This soaks the colour off the surface and back into the brush head – known as using a 'thirsty brush'.

All of the thin glazes are created with a solution of acrylic gloss medium, as well as water. However, rather than working into a pre-wet surface, texture/modelling paste is first applied to the paper and allowed to dry. Strokes of texture paste are directional, following the lie and form of the various elements within the composition and in some cases applied irregularly. Note that at the base of the mountain, for example, the paper is not fully covered. The uncoated paper produces darker areas, where the paper fibres absorb the colour more readily than the dry paste. Colours are as close to the first example as possible but here they flood the textures, to reveal their structure. All glazes were applied wet-on-dry in this case, the gradation of values achieved through adding more medium solution for lighter areas. However, the shoreline is treated differently, in that extra colour is stroked into the first thinly pigmented glaze.

Exercise

PREPARING AREAS OF HIGHLIGHT

The first area of highlights is produced with the help of masking fluid. This is applied to the areas which are to receive thin water-based washes of acrylic. The masking fluid is applied with a round soft brush, which can easily achieve detail or scuffs, as required by the subject. These will produce a purely visual textured highlight, using the surface as the white.

The foreground sheep and lamb however, have a layer of physical texture laid first. Here a bristle brush was used to build an impasto layer, using texture paste. The glazes applied here, run into the textures, leaving their prominences emerging as lights and later, highlights.

APPLYING WASHES

The top half of the painting is completed in thin fluid washes, mixing the paint with water alone. Several layers are applied slowly, wet-on-wet, building a range of values; often, to achieve added contrasts, more colour is added directly into the wet wash. Evidence of this is visible along the back of the foreground sheep, where the wash was deepened to allow the sheep extra contrast and a more prominent silhouette (negative painting).

The foreground sheep and lamb are painted with transparent glazes, with both water and medium in the mix. Here, colour is spread with a second brush, wetted with colourless medium solution. All colour was applied wet-on-dry in this instance.

Once again, two differing highlighting techniques are employed in this study, which demonstrates more complex mixing of colour by layers and the creative use of the contrast between a flat and an impasto surface. The sheep and lamb in the foreground, along with the small area of grass around them, are given some impasto texture using texture/modelling paste. Once dry, a second layer of the same is added to the lamb, giving it extra dimension. Again, allowed to dry, before the whole painting is coated with a thin layer of acrylic white paint. This ensures that colour washes are evenly absorbed across the whole surface of the painting.

Masking fluid is used to protect the highlights of the distant lambs, before painting begins. Each area is given several layers of transparent colour, but the foreground sheep and lamb are glazed, with medium added to the mix.

Finally, white is scuffed onto the sheep and lamb in the foreground, the only opaque colour applied in this demonstration. There are two reasons for doing this here. First to enable you to compare these whites to the white of the distant lambs, produced by the white of the watercolour paper. Second and most important of all, you will see the startling effect of opaque highlights scuffed over impasto glazing. These are perhaps one of the most exciting colours to lay, as they contrast directly with the accents in the glaze, deep in the impasto texture.

Common problems

PROBLEM

Absolute cleanliness and vigilance is essential when using brushes with acrylic paints. Many brushes are rendered useless simply through lack of attention, which is an unnecessary waste of brushes.

CARING FOR BRUSHES IN ACRYLIC PAINTING

If brushes are only partially cleaned a weak solution of acrylic paint may be left behind. Once the water evaporates off, the solution left in the brush becomes stronger and even a small amount will glue the hairs together into a solid lump. Far better to overwash brushes, than to risk losing them altogether.

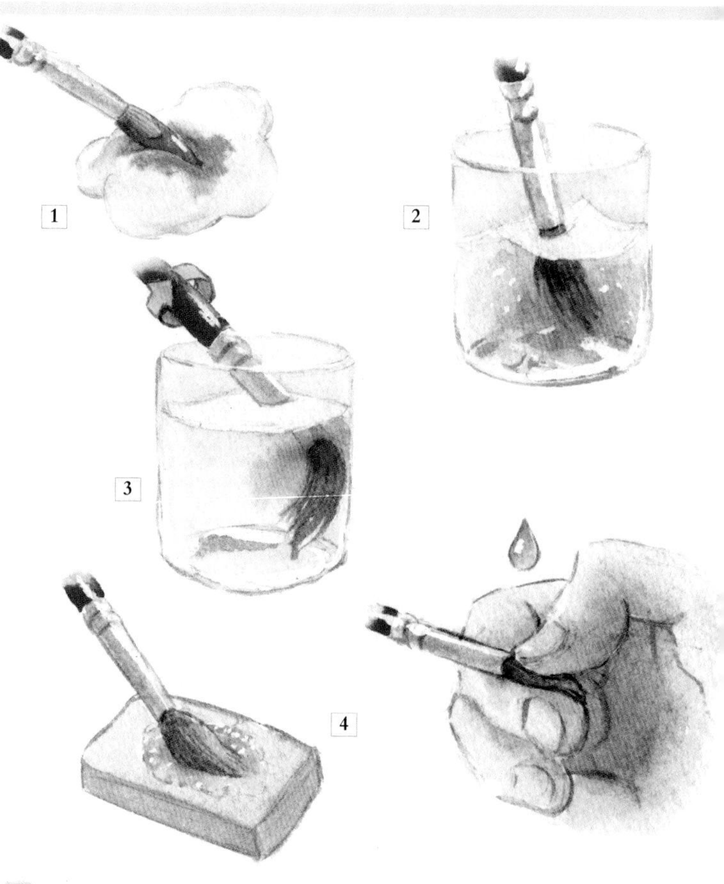

Fig. 1 Wipe the brush in an absorbent tissue to remove the bulk of any paint.

Fig. 2 Swish the brush around in a jar of clean water.

Fig. 3 To get paint out of the base of the brush hairs, push the brush head against the side of the jar and rotate gently.

Fig. 4 Remove from the jar and work soap into the hairs by rubbing them over a bar of soap, or dipping the brush head into liquid soap. Work the soap into the hairs with a fingernail.

Fig. 5 Place brush head back into jar of water, push against the side and rotate. Repeat these last two steps until you are confident that all traces of paint have been removed.

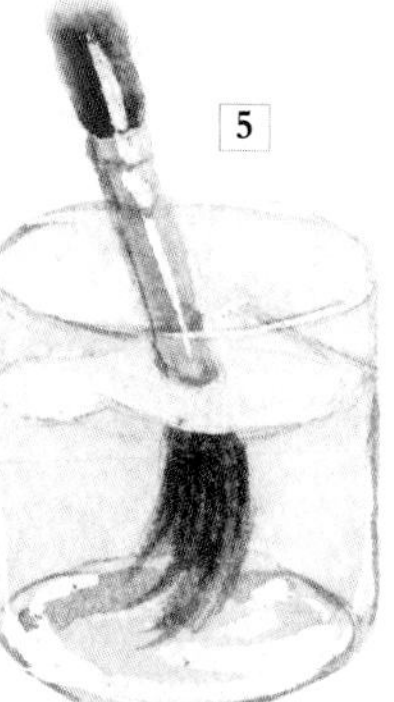

IMPORTANT

NEVER LAY A BRUSH TO ONE SIDE WITH EVEN A DROP OF ACRYLIC PAINT IN ITS HEAD. TRANSFER IT IMMEDIATELY TO A BRUSH WASHER OR THE WET SURFACE OF A STAY-WET PALETTE.

TIP:
Finally, rinse brush head under running water. Always used cold water to wash brushes, as hot water damages the brush head.

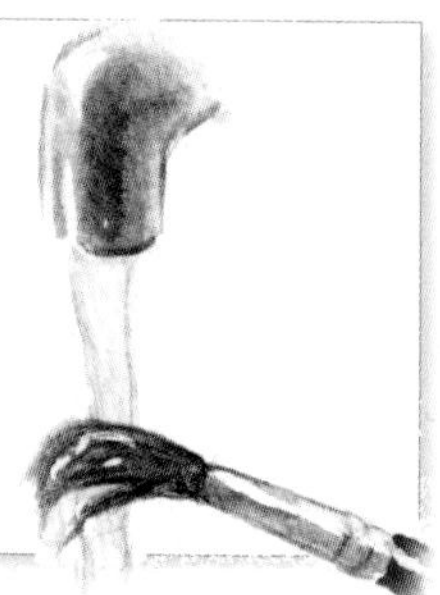

Discovering paint qualities

Each painting medium has its own particular strengths and acrylic paint is no exception. Notwithstanding the fact that many techniques from watercolour painting and oil painting can be brought into play.

This versatile medium therefore offers any painter the opportunity to exploit its full potential and develop a unique style based on one or more of its many merits.

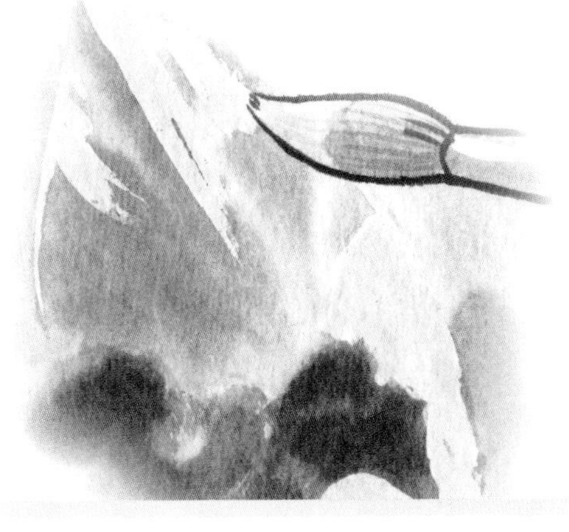

ACRYLIC PAINT CAN BE APPLIED FLUIDLY and transparently. Simply by adding water, it is possible to apply washes of colour to either a wet or dry surface. The added bonus in working with acrylics is the fact that when these gentle layers dry, they do so permanently and the colours are fixed. No matter how aggressive the application of subsequent layers, the colours beneath will not move.

Furthermore, while still wet, overpainted colours can be removed and corrections are possible, without disturbing the dry layers beneath. As a technique in its own right, this proves exceedingly useful. A passage of painting can be carried over an edge and wiped off, up to that edge. This technique is put to good use in the following exercise, in which the background is sharply arrested as it touches the glass bottle, defining the edge as it does so.

Fluid mixes are also created with acrylic medium, rendering them both transparent and more glutinous in consistency. This comes into its own when working upright, since it is important that a wash or glaze stays in place.

While letting the colour down with either water or medium makes it more transparent, you will at some point want to use the colour straight from the tube. Acrylic paints are available in different consistencies, from softer fluid colour to those suited to working with stiffer impasto acrylic layers. With the addition of varying quantities of white, the painter is also equipped with a range of opacities.

Both the exercise and stage-by-stage painting in this project maximise many of these aspects to the full. The ability to gradually work from light to dark, then back to light, offers an enormous range of values and qualities of paint surface. To have the facility to contrast a transparent area of paint against an opaque one, excites the eye and grabs the viewer's attention.

On top of all this, the intense hues of these paints provide acrylic painters with access to a palette of powerful glazes, with which to enrich colours and increase visual texture.

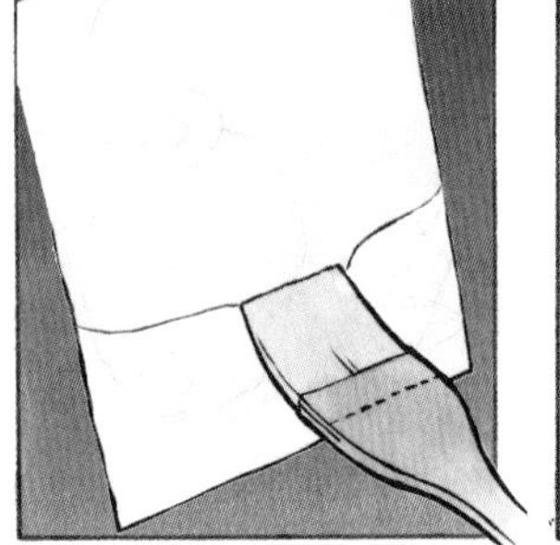

WET-ON-WET
THIN WASHES
Complete pencil drawing and use Hake to wet entire surface of paper.

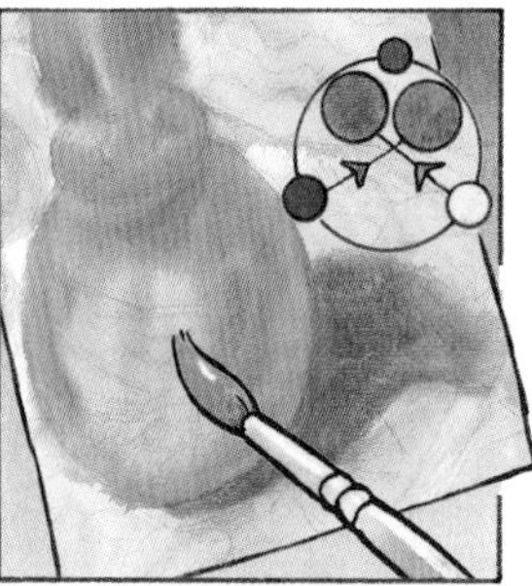

COMPLEMENTARY UNDERPAINTING - Apply fluid solution of colour with large round brush. Washes will flow into wet surface.

WET-ON-WET
STIFF BRUSH-STROKES
Use stiff mix to shape brush on the palette surface.

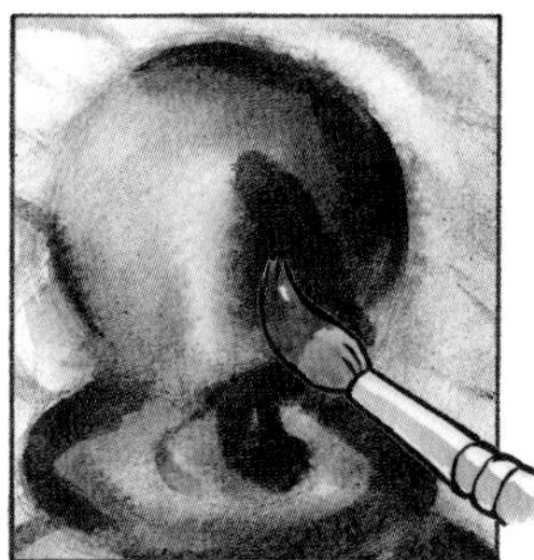

Rewet surface and apply soft dark wet-on-wet accents. Use round brush and apply paint as solid strokes of colour.

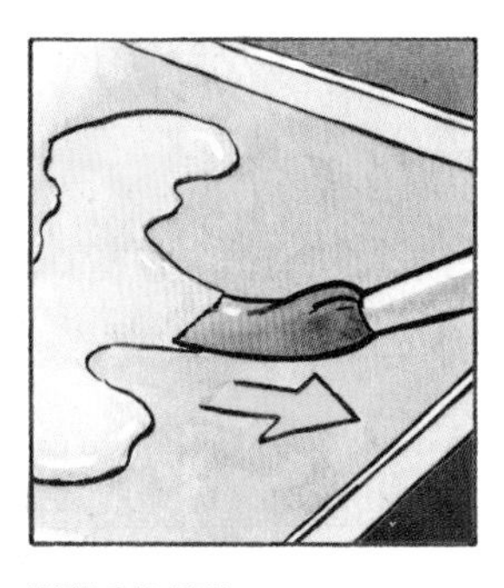

WET-ON-DRY
TUBE CONSISTENCY PAINT
Flatten damp round brush on palette surface.

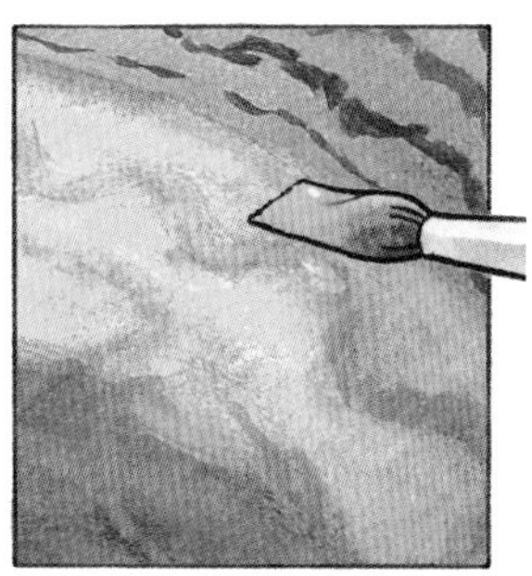

Use shaped brush to scuff colour onto dry surface to suggest texture of cloth.

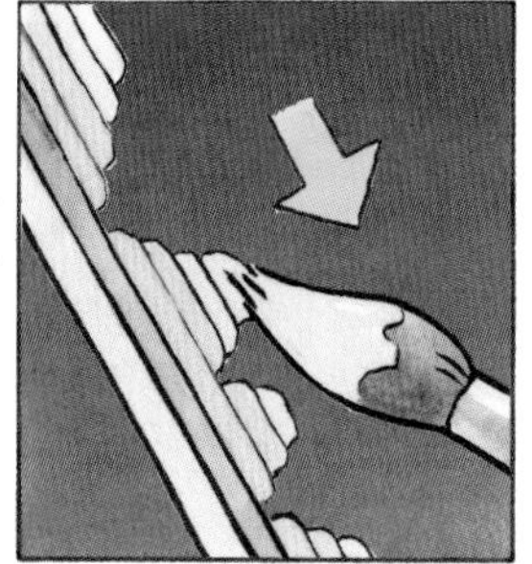

Apply paint in layers, scuffed over each other. Slowly build towards light. Keep coverage intermittent so all layers come into play.

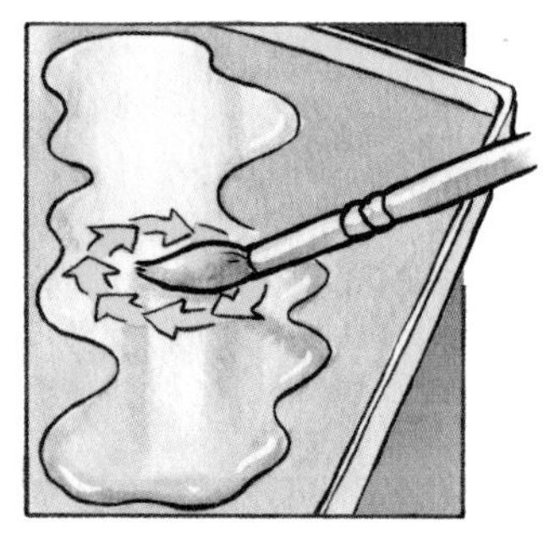

WET-ON-WET
TUBE CONSISTENCY PAINT
On separate area of palette produce solution of acrylic medium and water.

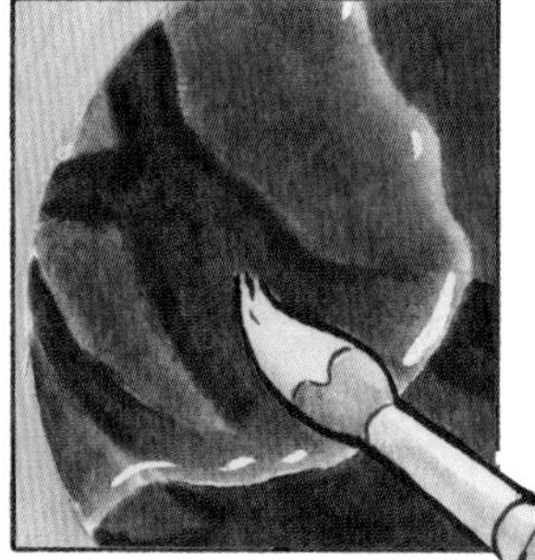

Brush a thin layer of the medium solution over the specific area to be painted.

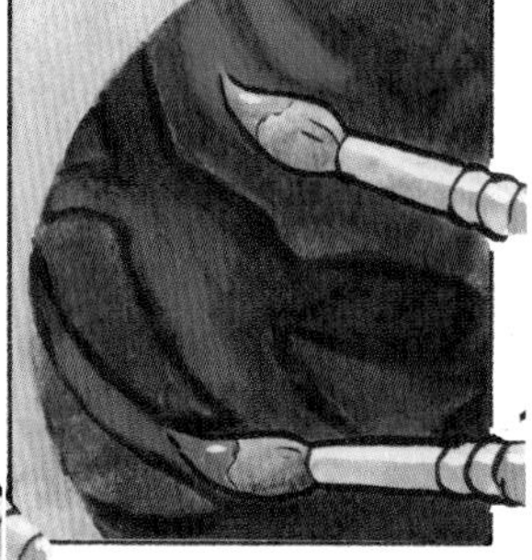

Brush tube consistency colour mixes directly into the wetted area, for soft opaque strokes, moving toward light.

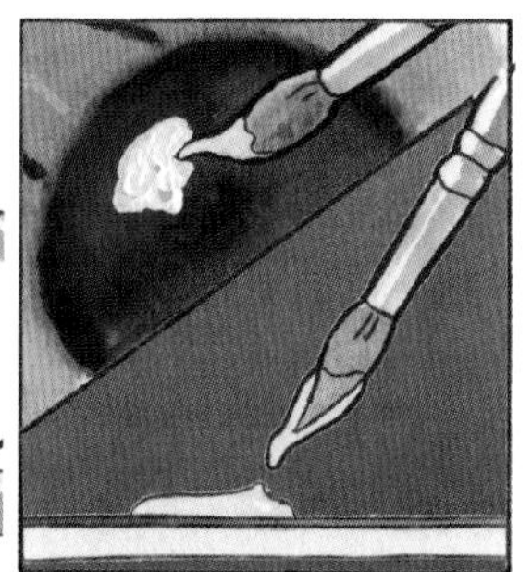

FINISHING TOUCHES
IMPASTO/ TUBE CONSISTENCY PAINT
Drip impasto highlights onto dry surface.

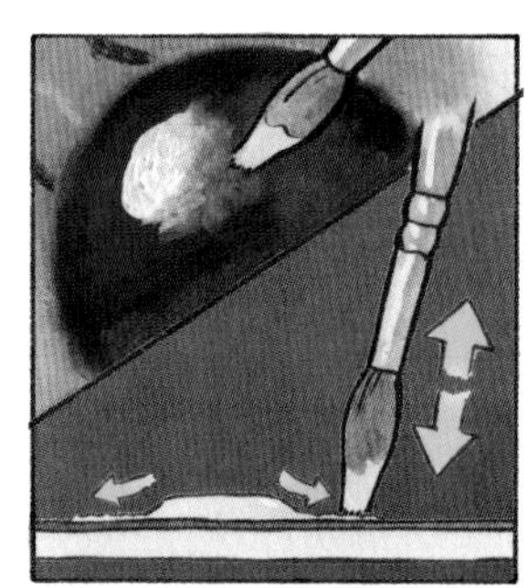

Dampen brush with medium solution and stipple edges of impasto to soften them

Exercise

The varied textures in this still-life make an ideal subject on which to experiment with different techniques and to exploit the many attributes of acrylic paint. A stretched piece of watercolour paper is required when working with the Wet on Wet technique.

The first stage involves the use of thin washes of colour. Unlike the method used in the basics section, there is no need for these washes to be rendered transparent, as they will be heavily overlaid with other colours. The purpose of the first stage is to simply define the composition and blank out the white paper surface.

The finished painting requires intense colours and will also benefit from exciting contrasts against which they can shine. Exploiting complementary colour washes at an early stage will imbue subsequently applied paint with these qualities. This involves the use of colour opposites on the colour circle.

CLOTH
Build wet-on-dry layers of colour for the yellow cloth and its stitching detail. Use scuffing and scumbling to both create texture and also to allow the viewer to see down through the built up layers of colour.

GLASS BOTTLE
Note the subtle colours of the glass. Unusually, although this is the centre of attention, it is painted primarily wet-on-wet, keeping it in soft focus until the final highlights are applied. In this instance, the overlaid wet paint layers are opaque, rather than transparent, building towards soft lights. In this area the surface is not simply wetted with water, but with a layer of medium solution, which softens and slows the colour flow.

HIGHLIGHTS TO GLASS
Working right through to pure white, these are still soft-edged, to impart the feel of its surface quality.

Stage-by-stage

NOTE

BOTH BACKGROUND AND LEAVES HAVE SOME OF THE FIRST LAYER SHOWING THROUGH, WHEREAS THE FLOWER HEADS ARE SOLID. THIS IS DELIBERATE AND SUGGESTS THAT THE FINAL FOCUS WILL BE ON THE FLOWERS.

THE AIM OF ANY FLOWER STUDY is to achieve a balance between softness and brilliance of colour. For this painting the two qualities are achieved in two distinct ways. The soft qualities naturally associated with flowers, will be attained through using the Wet on Wet technique. Bright colours are achieved with opaque colours, rendered wet-on-dry.

STAGE 1

Step 1 Work on a stretched piece of watercolour paper. Complete the initial pencil drawing. Begin the painting by generously wetting the overall surface, using a Hake brush. Switch to a large round brush to apply the background, and produce a fluid mix of blue grey. Only sparsely load the brush, so that the wash does not run too freely on the surface. Once completed, add a touch of yellow to the same mix to turn into a grey green for the leaves. Use more pigment to mix a very dull red purple for the flower heads, which need to be the darkest areas of this background layer. This is essential, for it provides the necessary contrast to offset the bright rich lights that follow.

Step 2 Having eliminated the majority of the white paper and allowed the initial colours to dry thoroughly, the balance of light and dark areas can now be reconsidered. The first colours are now stable and the surface is able to take a more aggressive layer of wet-on-wet. Wet the background in successive sections, as you paint. This allows more time for consideration, as a darker blue grey is selectively applied. Note how the leaf shapes were further defined at this point, by painting this background mix along their outer edges (negative painting). Once the background has been strengthened, move on to the leaves, rewetting them one by one. Apply darker green strokes, following the internal structure of each leaf. Once again, keep these dark and dull to provide the necessary contrast for the brighter opaque colours to follow. The flower heads are worked on in sections, wetting the surface before applying a cooler purple, brushed on to describe the structure of the fan-shaped trumpets and the frills on their top ridges.

STAGE 2

FLOWER HEADS

The dark purples of the flower heads need richer and deeper accents and should be treated to a glaze of red-purple. The glaze comprises acrylic gloss medium and pure colour, without the addition of white. Keep surplus water to a minimum, to ensure a deep and transparent, relatively stiff mix. When brushed generously over each flower head, the structure is kept intact, while the colour is deepened.

LEAVES

The leaves, on the other hand, begin to move back toward lighter colours for the sunlight, with the addition of opaque warm colour. To effect the suggestion of sunlight it is essential to add yellow to the colour mixes. However, the jump to this very yellow green may at first seem a little dramatic. Yet, this is precisely what such a structural flower image requires, particularly an exotic form such as this. The leaves need to be powerful and yet still allow the viewer's gaze to be concentrated on the flower head. Use the round brush, mainly side on, to brush the strokes along the leaves, following their structure. Use the point for detail and line at the edges. Keep a second brush handy, dampened with a water plus medium solution, to lose hard edges, where the light folds around leaf structures in shadow.

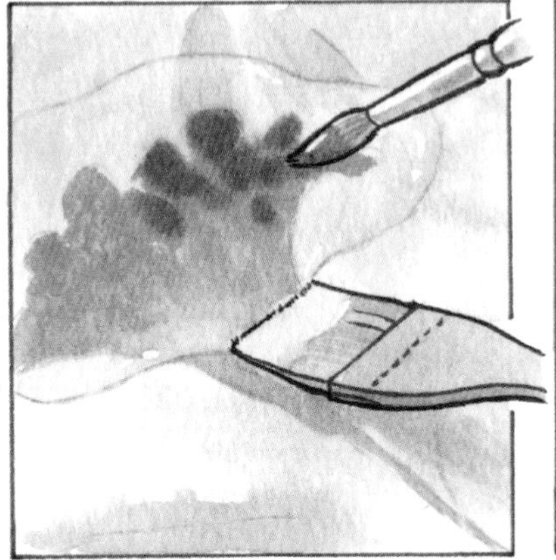

Working wet-on-wet with acrylic paints is simple, since dried underlying layers are permanent.

Once completed and allowed to dry thoroughly, glazes and opaque colours can be applied wet-on-dry and worked from dark to light.

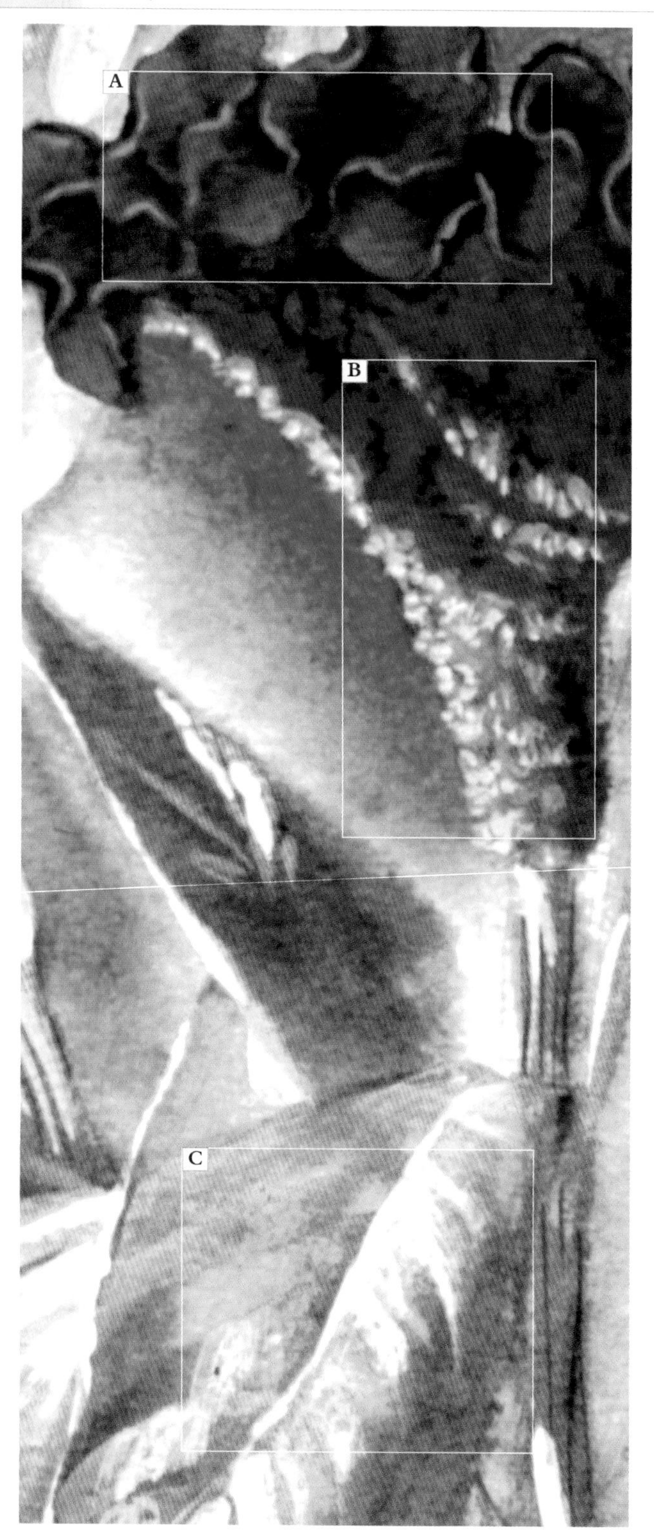

STAGE 3

Colours are nearly all applied at tube consistency at this stage, to achieve maximum intensity of colour.

Section A

The flower head frills form the focus of the study. This is where the most intense colours are applied and the strongest accents created in the depth of the flower. The highlights are also pure pigment, using yellow, rather than white, to provide the required value contrast.

Section B

Both shadow and sunlit areas are composed of purples. However those in shadows are cool (blue purple) and dark. In sunlight they are warm (red purple) and light. Shadows cast by the frills have a relatively sharp edge, against the softer edge of the shadow along the right hand side of the flower trumpet.

Section C

The cool greys of blue and green that form the underpainting are transparent and the lighter values are created from the white of the paper beneath. In contrast, the overpainted brighter yellow and yellow white hues are lightened by adding white to the mix, making them opaque. Such contrasts, lying in very close proximity, create visual interest to catch the eye.

LEAVES

The leap to the highlight colour is once again dramatic. The first mix, being a cool white, comprises white with a little added blue. The second, a warm white, comprises white with a touch of yellow. This effects the natural occurrence of reflected light (cool) and direct highlights (warm). The strokes need to be strong, drawn in the direction of the leaf shape and fading, where necessary, into a dragged scuff.

FLOWER HEADS

These are built towards light. For their unusual furry underbelly, move through increasingly cool purples, up to orange reds, for the warm effect of sunlight, finishing off with white highlights. In the frills, pure red is stroked into the curves of the petals to render the intense lights. Along the edges, through the addition of yellow to the mix, it becomes an orange curving line, applied with the brush point.

Common problems

PROBLEM

Taking care of tubes of paint is every bit as important as keeping brushes clean. Replacing caps immediately after squeezing out paint is critical, as is ensuring that caps and necks of tubes are clean of paint before replacing the cap. However, caps can become stuck fast.

Solution

It might be possible to remove the cap by gently twisting it off with a pair of pliers. However, if the cap is stuck fast there is the distinct possibility that this course of action would twist the tube. This is more than likely to result in it splitting open, the paint oozing out and the whole tube subsequently drying solid.

Fig. 1 Hold the cap under running hot water. This will expand the plastic of the cap, which should loosen it sufficiently to allow you to gently unscrew the cap.

Fig. 2 It is imperative that the tube is not twisted and torn apart and a simple little step should lessen the chance of this happening. Roll the bottom of the tube upwards to increase the pressure of the paint in the tube and squeeze as you unscrew the cap.

Fig. 3 Once the cap is loosened off, unwind the base and gently squeeze the side of the tube to restore its shape and release the pressure.

Fig. 4 IF THE CAP BECOMES TOO HOT TO HANDLE, SIMPLY WRAP SOME CLOTH AROUND IT.

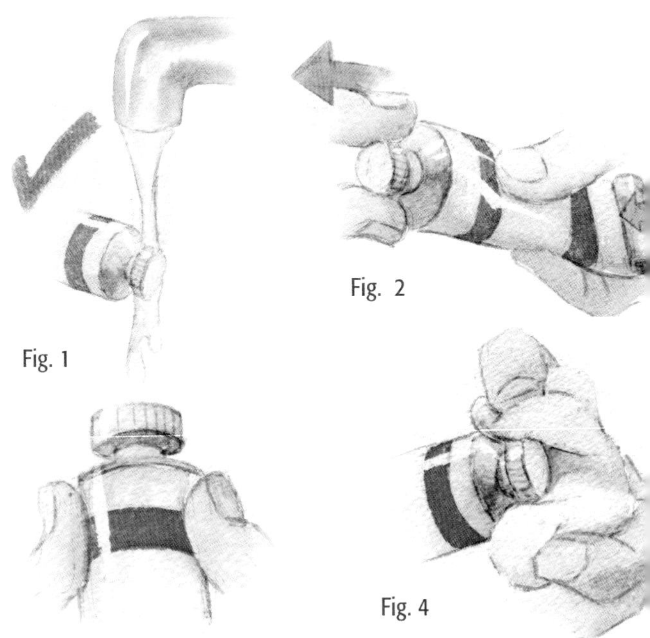

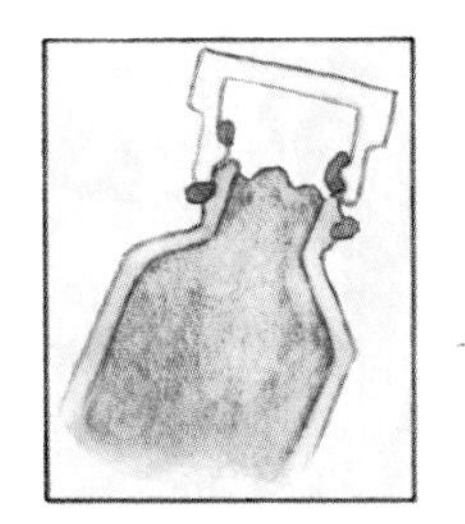

TIP: A plug of paint may form in the neck of a tube. The neck is the most prone to drying out, being closest to the air and containing such a small quantity of paint.

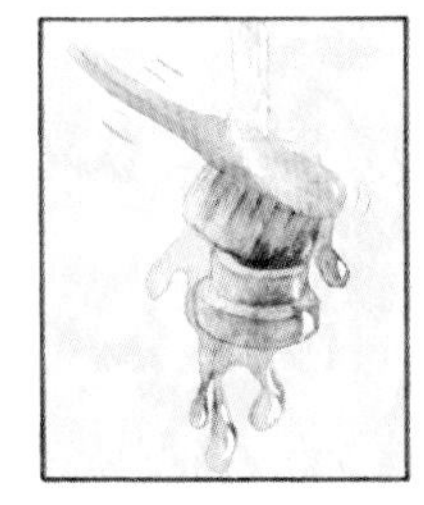

Caps must be kept clean. If paint in cap is wet, scrub it off with a small bristle brush, such as an old toothbrush.

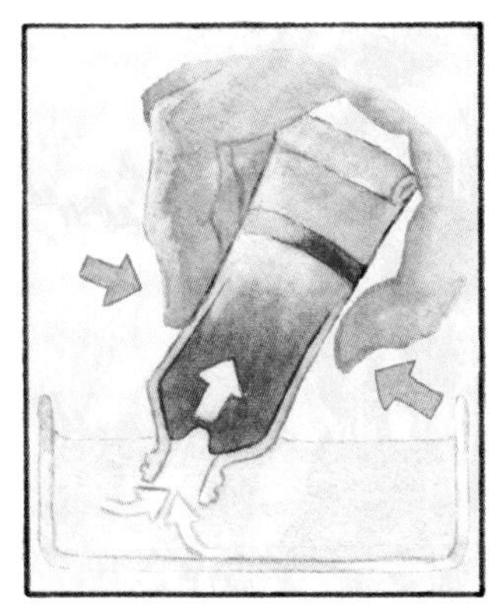

Before replacing cap, immerse tube head in clean water and gently squeeze side of tube. Paint will be pulled back into tube along with a small amount of water filling the neck. When cap is replaced the water remains in the neck, keeping the paint at the top of the tube fluid for a long time.

Exploiting brush-strokes

Acrylic paint is so strong that it could be applied with any tool, from a stick or a finger, to a large household brush. Since the paint needs no help in making it stick to the surface, the brushes with which it is applied must therefore fulfil another function.

In acrylic painting, brushes are used to imbue the paint with character. For this to be most effectively achieved, acrylic painters must fully understand the qualities of the paint and the nature of different brushes.

THE BRUSH IS THE INTERFACE between the artist and the painting. If it is not up to the job the painter cannot hope to succeed, particularly when working with such a versatile medium as acrylic.

Acrylic paints can take on the nature of thick oil paint, or fluid watercolour. Yet in reality, they are unlike either of these media. The consistency of acrylic paint in the tube lies between watercolours and oils. It dries by evaporation and as a result, loses some of its bulk. When applied with a brush this needs to be taken into consideration, for the resultant brush-strokes will inevitably flatten somewhat as the water dissipates.

When working with stiff mixes and in thick layers, the choice of individual brushes depends on how well they mix paint, load with colour and achieve surface textures. Brushes need to create enough depth of texture to overcome shrinkage, so that overpainted transparent coloured glazes can have an exciting surface in which to run.

On the other hand, working with techniques such as Wet on Wet, or with fluid washes, requires brushes that can wet the surface swiftly and evenly, brushes that produce soft brush marks without losing definition.

Most painters are quick to assume they are to blame when their painting goes awry. More often than not however, the problem lies with the tools, such as the incorrect brush being used for the job at hand.

For example, a much used technique is that of losing (softening) an edge. A stroke of colour is laid and while still wet, another brush- loaded merely with water or a colourless medium solution - is used to lay another stroke alongside. Colour from the first stroke bleeds into the wetted area to produce a lost edge.

For this technique to be successfully applied, the second brush needs to be soft and flexible, so that it does not disturb the first colour, while gently laying the colourless stroke.

Although it is not necessary to have a large range of brushes to begin with, it is essential that those you choose are of the right quality. It is far better to have good quality brushes and work with cheaper paint, than expensive paint that you are struggling to maximise with ineffectual brushes.

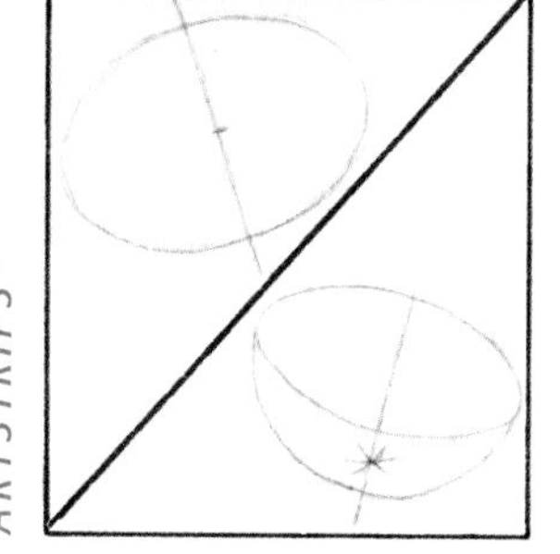

Most flowers are symmetrical in shape. Hold pencil against flower head, turn until the shape is cut into two perfect halves – this is the line of symmetry.

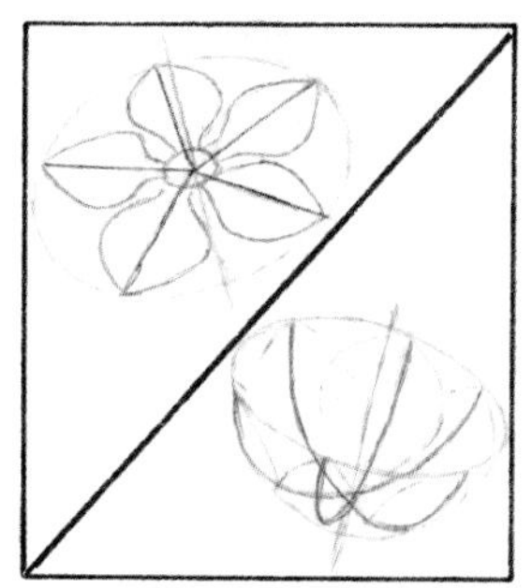

Petals now form on the flat ellipse or cup shape with elliptical top. The line of symmetry follows through into the stem connection.

Once completed, these curved petals belie their simple underlying structure.

This simple principle applies, even when flower heads appear in clusters or bunches.

Keep drawing loose and scribbly. Over detailing too early on may become lost under the heavy paint that follows.

Use bristle or stiff nylon brush to boldly block in dark colour. Add texture paste to the mix to provide body and substance in the paint.

Redraw with Rigger and fluid colour (add water and gloss medium). Draw rapidly to avoid getting bogged down in detail.

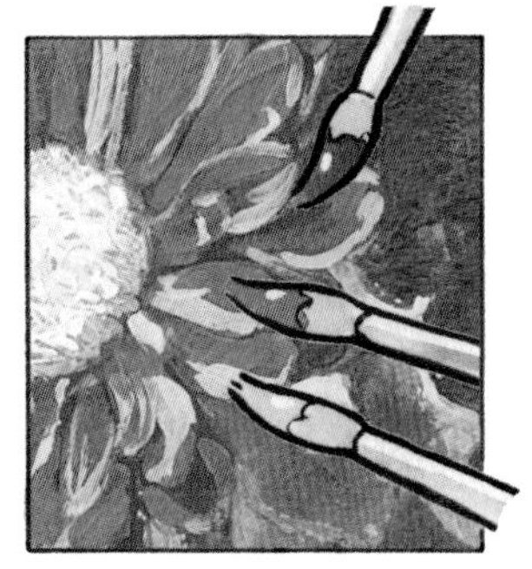

Use bristle brush and texture paste to build layers of lighter colour. To overlap petals naturally, start from back petals and work forward.

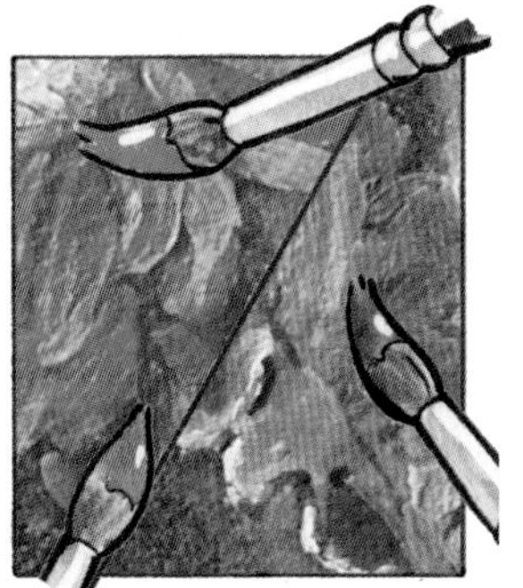

Switch to round soft brushes and apply glazes to enrich and darken underlying colours. Glazes are a mix of colour with gloss acrylic medium.

Apply blue and yellow tints over background and leaves to make them softer and recede. Tints are a mix of colour, gloss acrylic medium and white.

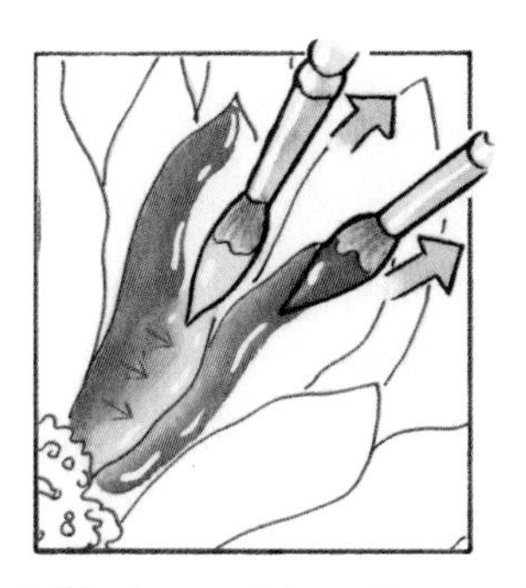

Build colours to light and lose some edges with a second brush wetted with gloss medium.

Drip on final highlights of pure white with a small round soft brush.

Exercise

The basic principle of this flower study is to use round bristle brushes to build up a brushy textured surface with stiff colour mixes. Once the base layers have dried, soft brushes are brought into play to modify the painting surface with layers of colour, glazes and tints.

Flowers are the ultimate subject with which to create intense colour and this powerful red is an excellent example. Flower petals are bright, even down into the darkest depths of their shadows.

Start the structural stage with stiff brushes, which are produced to handle heavy paint. In this instance, all of the colours for the first layer have been given extra body through the addition of texture/modelling paste. Once the impasto has been laid, clean your brushes thoroughly and refresh the palette in preparation for t he tube consistency colours and the enriching glazes.

Although tube consistency paint tends toward stiffness, round soft brushes can easily cope with building the paint from dark to light. These same brushes being used to render transparent and semi-transparent glazes and tints, before switching to a small round soft brush for the final highlights.

Coloured glazes are very important in this study, for they bring back the richness to layers that will have become chalky through the addition of white. Tints are used to render softness and depth, which are likely to have got lost in the build up of light values.

TIP: Although a Rigger brush could be used for the final highlights, a small round brush is better suited to dripping on the final, intense sparkling highlights.

Stage-by-stage

STAGE 1

Step 1 Round nylon brushes are used throughout, in the form of nylon 'bristle', nylon soft and nylon Riggers. Work on a stretched piece of watercolour paper. Use pencil to loosely define the composition and do not worry about mistakes, since the overlying opaque colours will be covering this initial pencil outline. Use a large round 'bristle' to block in the masses of the composition with dark, dull colours. Add generous amounts of carvable modelling paste to these mixes, which makes the paint much drier and stiffer and when applied, easier to modify on the surface. Cover most of the surface with vigorous brushwork, to create structural texture. Do not concern yourself too much with getting the right colours at this stage. The most important aspect of this layer is to obliterate as much of the white paper as quickly as possible. Allow to dry thoroughly, then re-establish the drawing, using a Rigger brush and fluid colour. Mix a dark colour with sufficient gloss medium to retain its strength, whilst also achieving the required fluidity.

NOTE

THE SKY COLOUR IS LAID AS DIRECTIONAL SWATHES OF IMPASTO COLOUR, WHICH WILL, ALONG WITH THE NEGATIVE PAINTING OF THE BRANCHES, FORM THE STRUCTURE OF THE TREE CANOPY, DURING GLAZING.

Step 2 Continue using the nylon bristle to build up thick textures, with colour over colour, working up towards the lighter values. Ensure that the undercolours are not lost entirely, but are allowed to come into play between the freshly laid brush-strokes. This mosaic of lighter strokes should not be over-mixed. Use a bristle brush to mix colour and carvable modelling paste, as before, but try to keep the colour mixes streaky, which will create more excitement in the end result. Since whites are being added to the colour mixes, they will begin to appear a little chalky. Allow this to happen, for at this stage it is the lightness of the colour mixes which are important, as they will inevitably darken, both on drying and with glazing. Fine detail such as the foreground grasses, applied with a Rigger, is further enhanced by scratching (sgraffito) or scraping (knife-work), after it has been laid. It is far easier to apply colour heavily and remove any excess.

STAGE 2

The bristle brushes and modelling paste have worked together to create an energetic surface, full of furrows and succulent strokes. These are now enhanced by flooding them with fluid colour or glazes, which are best applied with soft brushes.

The first colour mixes need to be kept transparent, by keeping white out of them. Mixes are created with gloss acrylic medium and enough water to make them really flow. Transparent glazes will reveal the grain of the surface, even discovering the structure within individual brush-strokes. Inevitably the colours also darken, but again, allow this to happen, as they will provide a contrast for the lighter colours of the final stage.

All the colours will now appear rather harsh and these can be selectively softened with tints, especially in the distance, to create a receding background. Tints are glazes, mixed as before, but with a little added white. By adjusting the quantity of added white, tints can be made semi-opaque, or semi-transparent.

When tinting, you need to take into account the fact that acrylic mixes become naturally more transparent as they dry. Consequently it may be necessary to apply a tint more than once, to achieve an effective semi-opaque result.

To prevent paint from drying in its temporary storage container during painting it is good practice to keep a pool or moat of water around the paint deposit. This can however cause a problem when mixing thick or opaque colour. Should the brush touch this water, a quantity will be drawn up into the brush head and interfere with the mix. Be vigilant; ensure the brush only touches the paint deposit.

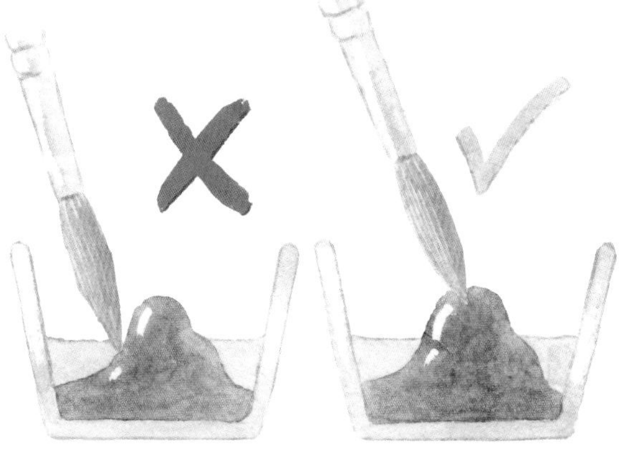

▷ **The textures created in the sky** are stained by dull purple glazes to suggest the platforms of fine branches. These are given a soft orange light by being scuffed over with semi-opaque colour. This richness of texture and glazes is very reminiscent of oil painting.

▽ **The building appears brighter** in contrast to the blue grey of the hill behind and the dark green of the bushes in front. It is one of the few places in the painting where white is used in its pure form and this draws our eye as if to a focal point. Note the semi-opaque brush-strokes, applied diagonally down the roof, gently suggesting the corrugated surface.

◁ **Scuffs and scumbles are used to maximum impact.** You can see right down to the dark underpainting, which now acts as tiny accents between the lighter strokes. Note how the textures change from directional strokes in the distance to more vigorous darks in the foreground and how they curve around the bales, to give them volume and form.

STAGE 3

For the final layers, continue to use the soft brushes, along with a Rigger. While the glazes enhanced the depths of the colours and the surface textures, these textures are now to be exploited quite differently. The aim is to apply lights and highlights without overwhelming the underpainting, by dragging brushes across the surface to produce scuffs and scumbles. A scuff is an individual paint stroke that catches the uppermost projects of a textured stoke within the underpainting. Scumbles are larger areas of applied scuffs. Brush-strokes are applied with the brush held at a very shallow angle to the surface, so that the paint mixes do not get into the furrows and depressions. Scuffs can also be made with transparent colour, simply by adding more gloss medium to the mix.

The continued presence of underpainting colours is essential for the finished quality of the painting; great care therefore needs to be taken not to overpaint at this stage.

Highlights on the buildings are achieved with pure pigment dripped from the tip of a small round soft brush, moving through to pure white. Foreground grasses and fence highlights are laid with a nylon Rigger. Note the hay bales, in which the reflected 'blue' lights are scuffed on top with a round soft brush. Their faces, which catch full sunlight, have warm orange yellow highlights dripped on.

Common problems

PROBLEM

It is all too easy when in the middle of an exciting passage of painting to set aside a brush with paint still in its hairs. This will have dire consequences, since it takes just a moment or two for the paint to dry and the brush-head to harden. But what to do if the flow of creativity is not to be interrupted?

Solutions

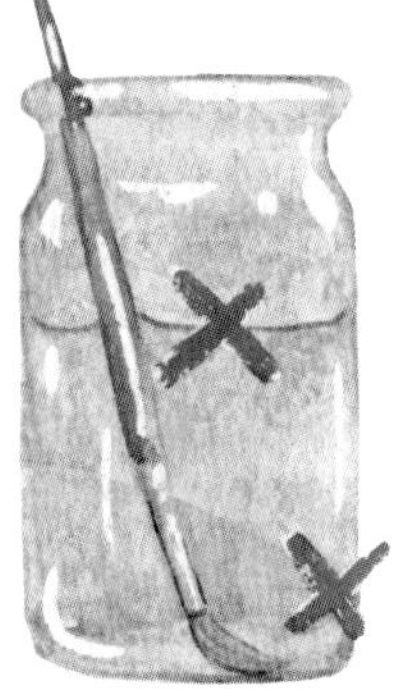

Although seemingly the simplest solution, to drop the brush into water is not the ideal method, since a brush left standing on its head in water for any length of time, will suffer damage to its shape and pointing capabilities.

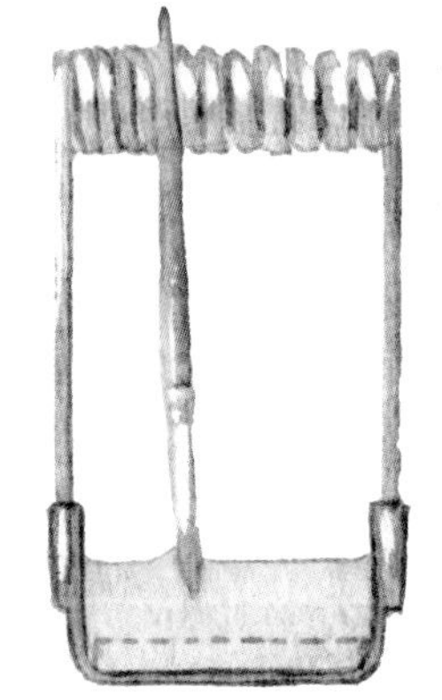

There are several better options. One being to use a brush washer, in which the brush is suspended head down from a coiled grip. Only the tip of the brush hairs hang below water level and the rest of the brush-head absorbs water by capillary action. Thus the brush retains its shape and the point.

Another option is a welled brush washer, in which the brush nestles into a groove, yet again with only the tip being in contact with the water.

These previous methods do involve the use of yet more equipment, both of which need to be kept at a safe distance, to reduce the likelihood of being knocked over. A shallow dish of water could prove a safer alternative, but again as with the others, offers space for a limited number of brushes.

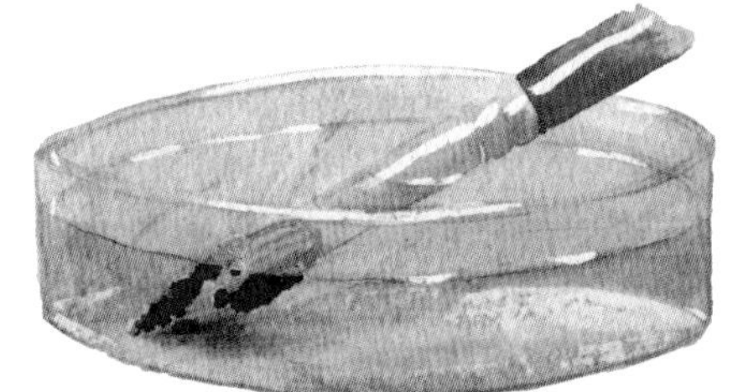

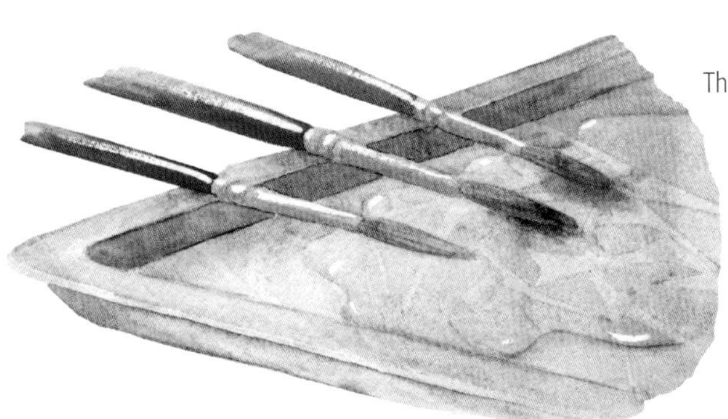

The simplest method by far is to keep the brushes within the vicinity of your palette, much as you would when painting in oils and in water-colours. Lay the brushes on the palette with the brush-head in direct contact with the wet surface of the stay-wet palette. The brush-heads will be kept moist through water seeping up into the hairs.

Should too much potential mixing surface be taken up, put together a dedicated stay-wet palette, kept specifically for the purpose of protecting brushes in use.

Exploiting palette mixing

Handling paints that are fast drying and which can be used either transparently or opaquely, requires a careful regime of palette control.

What exactly should the paint consistency be - wet or dry, thick or thin?

Should the paint be mixed with water or medium and should this be done on the palette or on the painting surface?

THE EXERCISE, SKETCHES AND ARTSTRIPS in the basics section on palettes helped you to become familiar with how to create colour mixes on the palette surface. Those mixes were generally produced for use in techniques akin to those of watercolour painting. In spite of the use of white and, in some cases, of stiff consistency paint, layering was carried out from light towards dark.

For the following exercise and painting project, you will be experiencing a much more powerful approach, one that has everything in common with techniques used in oil painting.

Layering from dark to light, in which the first layers cover the ground with dark, dull colours. As opposed to the white paper surface for the watercolour painting approach, this method uses dark acrylic paint to form the undercolour layer. Light opaque colours will be laid over this undercolour, with the addition of final intense colours applied as transparent glazes.

Each layer requires different consistencies of paint, which are mixed on the palette.

For this you will need to develop the ability to judge when to add water, when to add medium and when the paint can be used straight from the tube. These adjustments are made on the palette before the colour mixes are stroked onto the surface of the painting and each will load differently onto the brushes with which they are being applied.

As with all aspects of painting, this understanding can only be developed through trial and error. Use these tutorials as a guide and a challenge to help you gain control over the colour mixes on your palette. It is not the end result that matters; rather it is the process of striving to build up your understanding of the various techniques.

As the layers of paint are being built up, you will become familiar with how the composition of mixes for wet-on-wet painting is different to that required for wet-on-dry. You will better understand the advantages and disadvantages of spreading the paint mix as a thin or a thick layer on the palette. Even brush loading, for if this is not correctly controlled, it will not produce the desired result, no matter how skilled the artist.

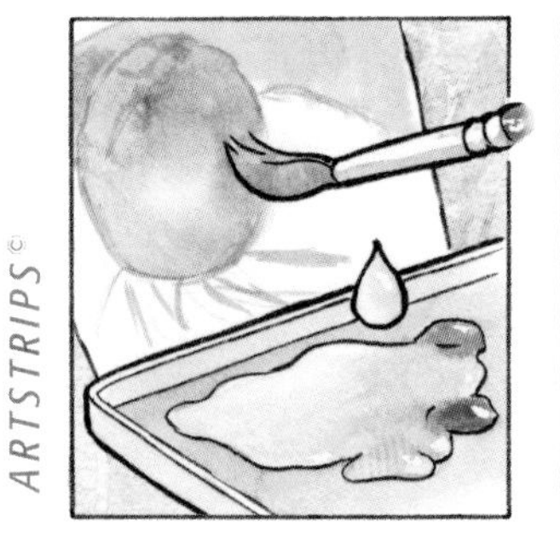

ELIMINATING WHITE GROUND Use fluid washes of colour to block in composition (add plenty of water). Do not over worry about hues or values.

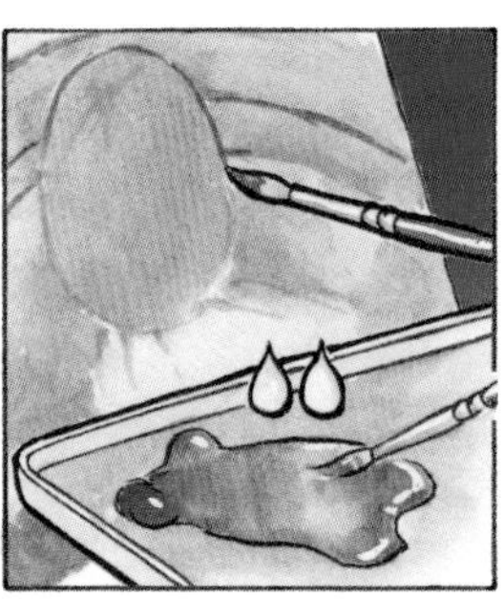

REDRAWING Create darker mix, using less water and a little medium. Redraw where necessary.

WET-IN-WET Deposit a pool of gloss medium onto the palette surface…

…add an equal amount of water and mix well, using a large round soft brush.

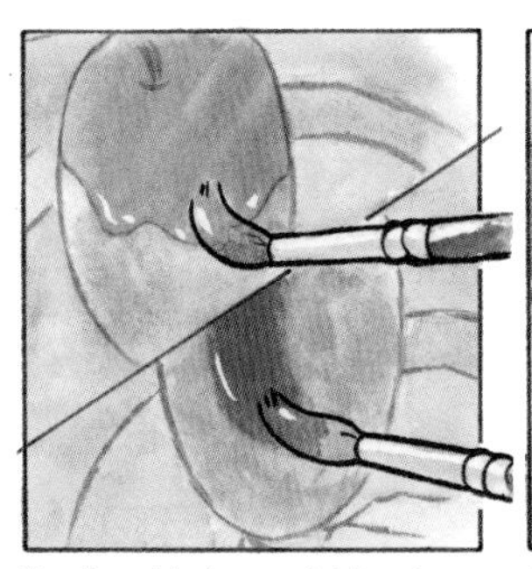

Brush a thin layer of this mix onto the area to be painted. Apply colour mix to this wetted area, for wet-in-wet strokes.

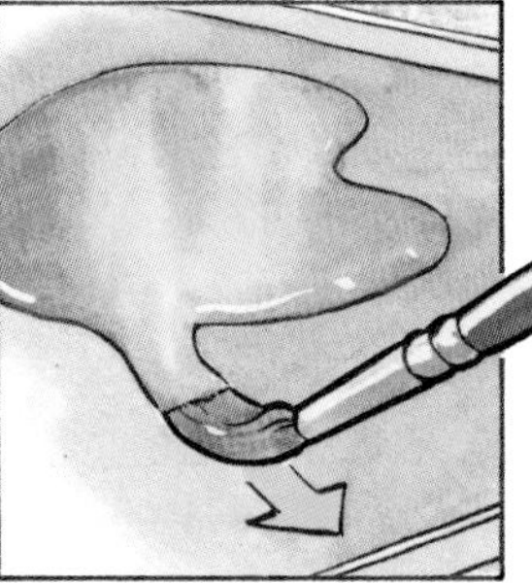

Flatten the round soft brush on the palette surface during loading...

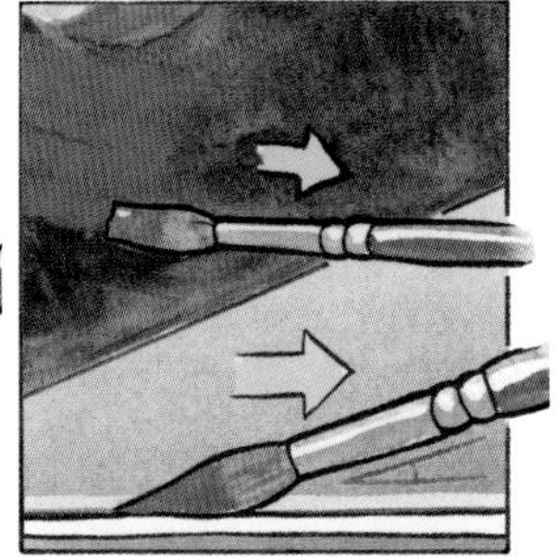

...so that colour is deposited evenly and swiftly from the flattened brush face. Keep brush at a shallow angle to the painting surface.

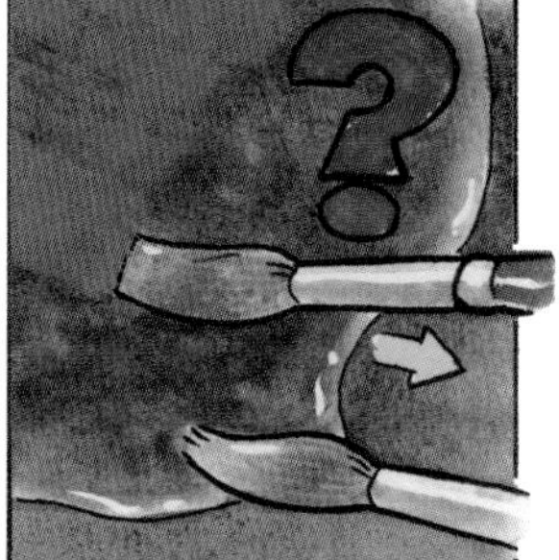

BLENDING HARSH BRUSH-STROKES Brush-strokes may still finish with hard edges and require blending.

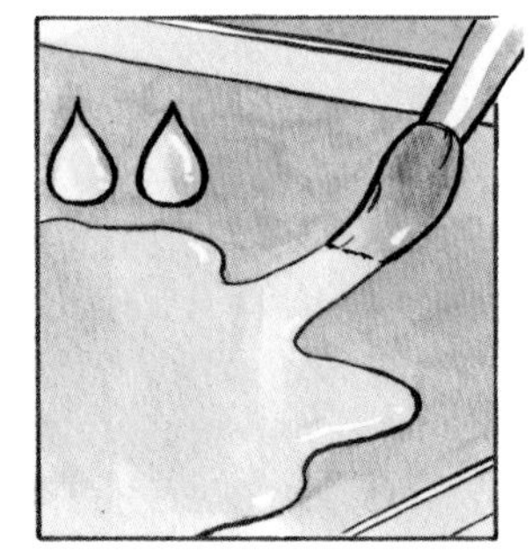

Dampen a clean round soft brush and gently load with the medium mix. Flatten brush head by pulling over palette surface.

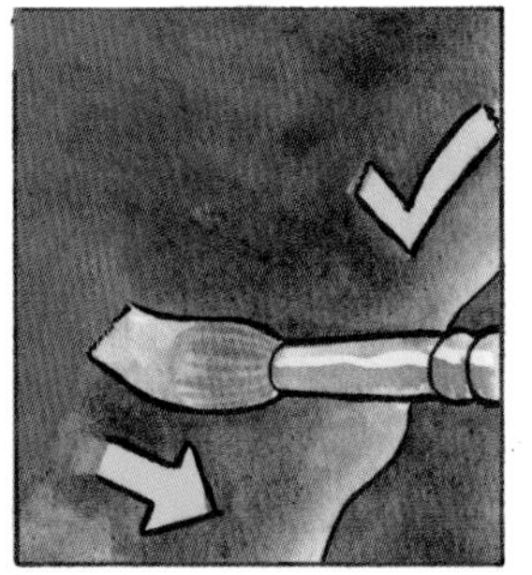

Return to harsh edges on the painting. Use the brush with medium mix to blend these edges so they soften as required.

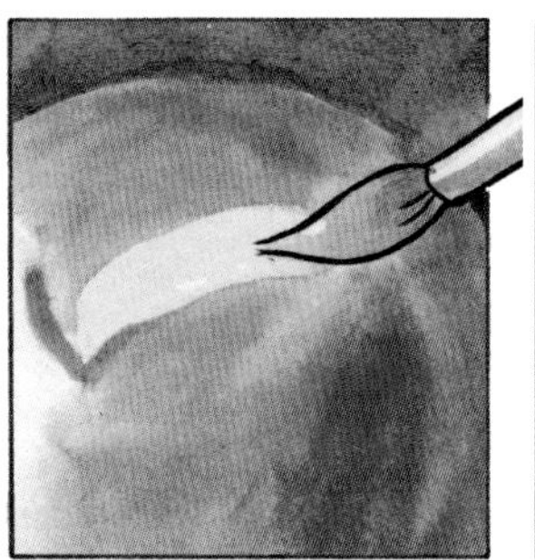

FINAL LAYERS Switch to wet-on-dry to apply light and highlight values to complete the painting.

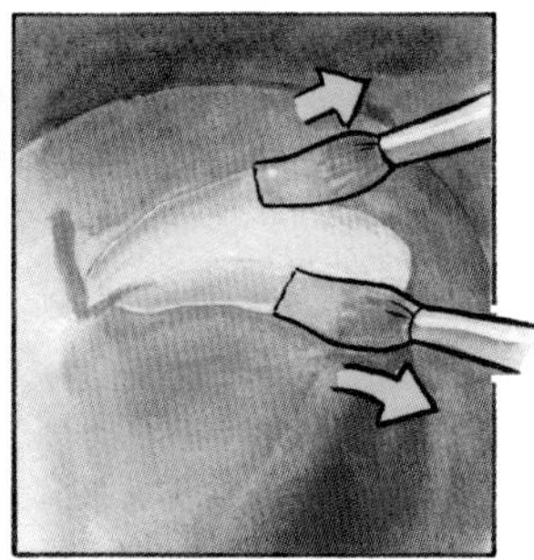

Use the blending technique with medium to soften any unwanted harsh edges of these highlights - before they dry.

Exercise

The most dramatic lighting for a still-life is to use an artificial source coming in from the side. This will really bring out the volume of your subject and provides strong shadows. However, these shadows can, on occasion, be too solid and this is corrected by reflecting a little light into them, through placing a piece of white paper or card on the opposite side of the still-life. This needs to be moved about until it reflects the light into the deep shadows at the desired degree and angle.

This relatively small painting was produced on a spare piece of acid-free mounting card, primed with white acrylic gesso primer. Look carefully and you will be able to see the surface of the card has a gentle texture not unlike that of smooth canvas, which is quite pleasing to the eye.

The object of this exercise is to firstly establish the darks of the painting, for which you will need to create complementary paint mixes. This use of complementary colour mixes also keeps the colours dull.

Rich darks behind the apple are further enhanced by being layered in successive cool and warm mixes. Such transparent darks are full of colour and complement the lighter brighter colours of the apples.

Several layers of the lighter colours are needed to finally achieve the values required. Note however, how the dark and middle values can still be seen below these lightened areas. The secret being, as always, when layering dark to light, never completely cover the colours beneath.

Finally, intense colours such as the bright reds of the apple (to which white had to be added to bring them to the correct value), need to be glazed.

COLOUR REFERENCE

Red-purple	[Rp]
Red-orange	[Ro]
Blue-purple	[Bp]
Blue-green	[Bg]
Yellow-orange	[Yo]
Yellow-green	[Yg]
Titanium White	[TW]

COLOUR MIXING

Where the pre-fix letter is shown in capitals this denotes a larger quantity of that particular colour.

Conversely, where the pre-fix letter is shown in a lower case, this denotes a smaller quantity of that particular colour.

Example:
Bp = **large** amount of blue-purple
bp = **small** amount of blue-purple

NOTE

GLAZING – A MIX OF GLOSS MEDIUM WITH COLOUR (AVOIDING WHITE), PROVIDES THE NECESSARY RICHNESS TO INCREASE THE DEPTH OF THE PREVIOUSLY LAID COLOUR.

Stage-by-stage

STAGE 1

This project will take you through palette mixing for both Wet on Wet and Wet on Dry paint application. The palette of colours required to complete this encompass complementary underpainting, warm and cool colour temperature overlays and tonal building of colour. Although this may sound ambitious, each step leads naturally and simply to the next and your experience of palette mixing and usage will be greatly extended and improved.

Step 1 The composition is gently drawn in with a 0.5 automatic pencil onto previously stretched, medium weight, watercolour paper. This initial drawing can be loose and extensive, since errors and heavy re-working will be easily covered by the paint.

At first the subject may seem complex, but the secret is not to worry about detail. Keep in mind the basic rhythms of the composition - for instance, the boats, which sweep down in a curved mass from top right to bottom left. Watch out for the negative shapes of the water in the foreground and to the left of the boats. It is far more important that you get these large areas balanced. The space of the water in the foreground is especially important, as it is to carry the colour of the boat reflections.

Detail can be added as the painting progresses. Note how the distant horizon line, which could cut the painting right across, is punctuated by the vertical masts, which act as stops to the viewer's eye.

Step 2 At this point the painting has the appearance of quite a pleasant line and wash watercolour, but this is deceptive. The colours are all applied wet-on-wet, with the surface first wetted using the Hake brush. They appear harmonious because they are all dulled with a little of their complementaries in the mixes. For example, oranges have blue added to turn them into browns. Many mixes also contain white, which serves to soften and dull their intensity. What is more, the overall colour of each area is complementary to the colour that is required in the finished result. The palette mix for these thinned down colours comprises colour, water and a little medium. White is added to give them body.

REDRAWING Prepare a dark mix of complementaries [Bp+ro+yo], using more gloss medium and just a touch of water to produce a dark, yet fluid mix. With a Rigger brush, use this mix to draw and re-establish the elements within the composition. The purpose of this redrawing is to act as a guide, which will free you up to be bold in your approach with the paint layers to follow. The dark line-work will show through the paint for some time, until the final opaque lights and highlights cover it at the end of the painting. Keep the line-work loose and if mistakes do bother you, simply wet the offending line and dab it off with an absorbent tissue, before it dries.

STAGE 2

The painting is now made darker overall, especially in the foreground, where these colours will provide the accents of the final painting. The palette mixes are much stiffer, their consistency adjusted by the addition of medium, rather than water.

Paint strokes are to be laid wet-on-wet. Each section of the painting is re-wetted independently, as it is to be painted. Start at the top of the painting to reduce the chances of water runs travelling across newly painted areas, resulting in the colours being lifted.

For the same reason, alternate the areas to be rewetted, in order that freshly laid paint in one area is not disturbed by the re-wetting of an adjacent area.

Colour mixes now move toward the final local colours, but still have a lot of their complementary colours added. This makes them generally dark and grey. Compare the colours of the greens on the hill and the water of the foreground to their final colours in the finished painting.

Not only are these colours dark at this stage, they also differ in colour temperature. The trees, painted blue-green in this layer, will have warm yellow-greens laid over them. On the other hand, the water darks are now painted warm purple and will eventually have cool blue and green laid over them. This variation in colour temperature makes the surface visually exciting and the colour much more realistic than simple flat greens and blues.

The overall dark balance of values of this layer is now ready to provide the contrast for the lighter colours which will help to create the sensations of afternoon sunlight.

In spite of the perceived complexity of the composition, it is, in fact, based on two basic elements.

(1) The two curved lines which contain the boats moored along the harbour [brown line]. The depth and width of this curved area can be adjusted, before any boats are introduced, so that it best fits the rectangle of the painting.

(2) The perspective of the boats [green lines]. Perspective is not an area of consideration to be feared. In fact, here you can see that it provides a series of diagonal movements through the moored boats. These lines appear to converge toward a point outside and to the left of the painting. This simple fact provides dynamism to the drawing and painting which one of the underlying strength of the composition.

STAGE 3

Since the values of this stage become lighter, the mixes need to contain added white. This makes them both opaque and slightly dull.

You need to take into consideration the fact that the colour in the palette mix will become darker as it dries on the painting surface. The medium in the paint is semi-opaque while wet, but dries to complete transparency. Thus, the less white present in the palette mix, the darker the resultant colour on the painting surface and furthermore, the greater its degree of transparency, which will allow the dark underpainting to show through.

The white's effect on the intensity of the colour mix must be accepted as you build the values lighter and lighter. It is much more important to increase this range of values, for without it you can effect neither volume nor light.

The dulling effect of the white on colours is not catastrophic, as the original colours can be restored through glazing. For glaze mixes, add a touch of the relevant colour to a pool of medium, keeping white out of them. On this painting glazing was used to restore the colour of the water, especially in the distance, where light, but bright scuffs of blue were required.

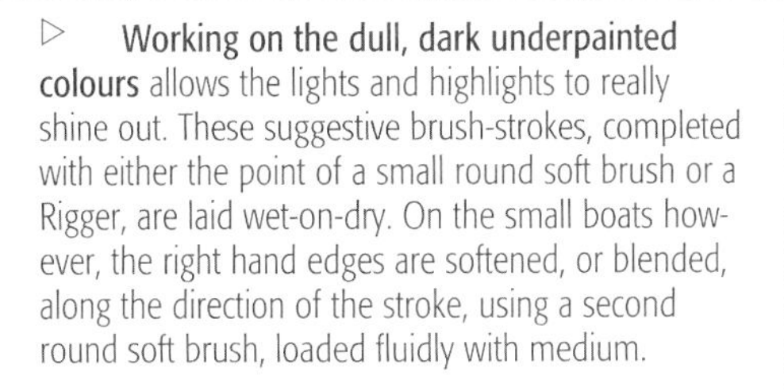

▷ **Working on the dull, dark underpainted colours** allows the lights and highlights to really shine out. These suggestive brush-strokes, completed with either the point of a small round soft brush or a Rigger, are laid wet-on-dry. On the small boats however, the right hand edges are softened, or blended, along the direction of the stroke, using a second round soft brush, loaded fluidly with medium.

▷ **Using white as a colour in these areas** would be impossible without the underlying blue-greys. As the white is laid layer on layer, the undercolours that remain untouched naturally become the shadows. The thickest layer (broad prows to the left) becomes the brightest white and the strongest highlight.

▷ **Look at the range of values in the foreground**, from the pure white of the light catching the rail of the boat to the dark accents of the water. These contrasts, brought so close to each other, really make our eyes feel that we are observing light. The effort put into creating the underlying layers pays dividends at the end of the painting and is worth all of your patience.

Common problems

PROBLEM 1

Over-dry Palette

Keeping palette mixes at the correct consistency can prove a problem due to the constant evaporation of water from the palette surface.

Soloution 1. With very fluid mixes this problem is usually minimal, since there is so much water present in the mix. For more solid paint strokes however, the paint has to be kept together as a deep deposit; even more so for mixes containing texture/ modelling paste, when the colour can be built up to quite a depth on the palette surface. The top layer of the paint on the palette thus becomes so removed from the wet palette that it is likely to dry and create a crust, which will prove irritating.

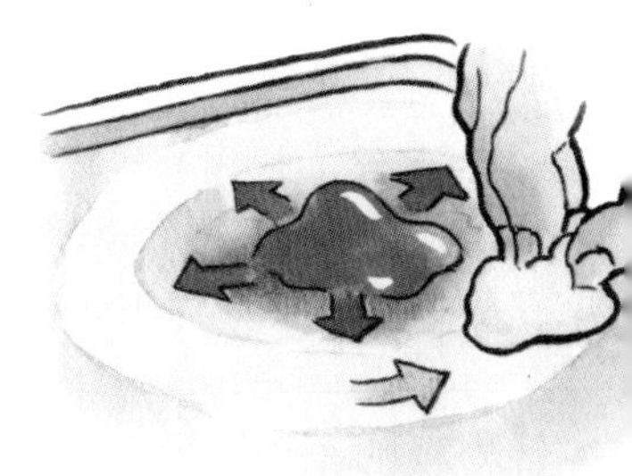

Use a plant mister, filled with water, to gently douse the palette mix. It is critical to ensure the mix is misted with water, rather than liberally sprayed, as the mix can go the other way and become too fluid. This treatment could prove beneficial when mixing on a dry palette, since the dry palette mix does not of course receive any water from the palette surface.

PROBLEM 2

Over-wet Palette

Having just loaded the stay-wet palette with water at the beginning of a painting session, it is common to suffer from an overload of water on the palette surface. Mixing on the fresh top sheet usually results in the paint becoming too fluid. This not only begins to run in all directions on the palette surface, but the mix is also too thin for powerful application.

Soloution 2 To overcome this, gently wipe the newly laid top sheet of the palette surface with an absorbent tissue. The mopped surface is still damp enough to keep the paint wet, but not overly wet to dissolve the paint deposits. Should you forget to do this and find that colour mixes begin to spread, use an absorbent tissue to carefully wipe around the paint deposit, or colour mix.

PROBLEM 3

Over-mixing Glazes

When mixing transparent glazes, only small amounts of glazing colour are actually required. However, adding sufficient medium results in a copious amount of a particular glaze mix, most of which is not required.

Soloution 3 To cut down on wastage Place the pool of medium on the edge of the palette surface, but leave sufficient space around it to deposit small amounts of the base colours. Draw tiny amounts of an individual colour into the edge of the medium, until you achieve the desired amount of glaze colour.

PROBLEM 4

Over-mixing with Whites

Mixing whites into colours can result in exactly the same problem, since acrylic pigment is extremely powerful. To achieve the desired light tint often results in large amounts of colour mix being wasted.

Soloution 4 To avoid this, adopt the same principle as for mixing glazes and always add the base colour to white at its edge, rather than white to the colour.

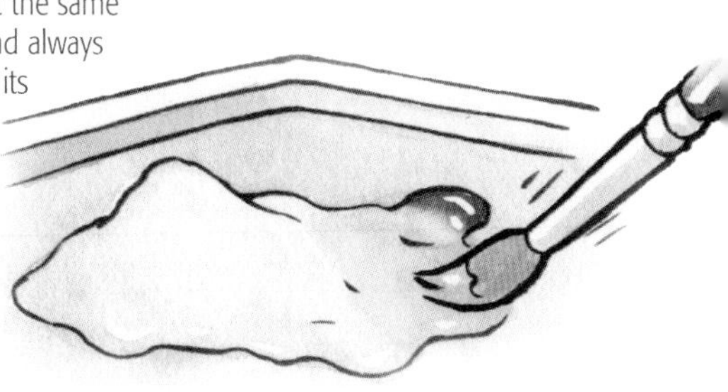

Discovering surface texture

In its natural form, acrylic paint tends to produce a rather flat surface and works well on smooth paper, card or wood panels. On these surfaces the paint can be layered as transparent and/or flat opaque washes, creating visual textures in the process. The strength of the medium ensures that even the thinnest of layers will adhere securely to such smooth surfaces.

ON THE OTHER HAND, IF TEXTURES ARE REQUIRED, acrylic paints will readily adapt to suit a particular rendition or required finish. Since the paint itself is not especially suited to produce impasto, it can be made so, by either adjusting the paint or the surface on which it is to be applied.

The paintings featured in this project show the surface being manipulated to achieve varying degrees and qualities of physical texture.

First to be explored - the possibilities when using a paper surface. Watercolour paper is available in a plethora of different surfaces, from rough to smooth and in a variety of thicknesses. Whether thick or thin, the paper will need to be stretched, for as the paper absorbs water from the acrylic paint, it will inevitably cockle, which would prove irritating in the extreme.

The surface quality of paper can be bolstered and in this instance texture/modelling paste is used to not only provide a better tooth to which the paint will adhere, but also for achieving directional physical strokes, to suggest structure.

Paint is applied in fluid form with the addition of water and acrylic gloss medium. As a consequence, both watercolour and oil painting techniques can be brought into play, while at the same time achieving a result that is unique and singular to acrylic painting.

Canvas boards provide a quite different surface on which to begin. In the first instance, they possess a surface that is already primed. Secondly, the surface texture of canvas boards features the weave of the canvas. In of itself, this provides a texture that can take scuffing and scumbling with ease.

When texture paste is directly applied to the surface of a canvas board, the regularity of the weave is interrupted and manipulated to better suit the needs of the subject. This potential is exploited in the painting that takes as its subject a tiger's head emerging from the bush.

Surface texture can be furthered through brush-strokes and with unusual techniques such as tonking. Primarily conceived as a method for soaking excess oil from the surface of an oil painting, tonking is exploited to bring out textural qualities in fluid paint. This method is used to a considerable degree to achieve visual impact in the stage-by-stage painting.

Exercise

This study of a section of the wall shows exactly how the surface texture is exploited to create the effect of sunlight and shadow. Although the texture travels through areas of fine detail, such as in the birdcages, it must be overcome to capture their essential fragility with fine overlaid line-work.

1. PRE-TEXTURED SURFACE

The ground for this exercise is stretched smooth watercolour paper, on which the composition is drawn in strongly with a 2mm 2B pencil. Texture/modelling paper is brushed onto the surface with a large, stiff nylon brush. Add a touch of colour to the paste to make it more visible when applying the strokes. With so little pigmentation in the paste it will dry more or less transparent, allowing the underlying pencil work to show through. The whole surface is to be covered with thin colours, through which the strong underlying drawing will continue to be visible. Use a flat nylon brush to flood fluid washes of colour (colour and water) across the texture. The thin colours will flow into nooks and crannies, discovering not only the texture, but also the bare paper areas, which will become the darkest areas of paint.

2. WASHES AND LINE-WORK

Apply a second layer of fluid washes to bolster the first – washes of colour and water. To render the pigmentation more interesting, overlay washes in alternating colour temperatures. Observe how the walls have a purple wash overlaying the previously laid blue. Alternating, uneven applications of colour at this stage will mean that considerable variations of colour mix will exist across the surface. Switch to a large Rigger brush and begin to introduce line-work rendered in paint, to establish some of the fine detail. Use a fluid mix of colour using water and colour, but add more pigment. Keep the drawing as loose as possible. The Rigger and fluid paint will enable you to keep the approach relaxed and the colour still relatively transparent.

3. WORKING BACK TO LIGHT

Water is now reduced within the colour mixes and acrylic gloss medium used in its place. This renders the mixes more viscous, which enables the colours to be scuffed and scumbled across the surface texture much more easily. Load a large round brush with stiff yellow white mixes and flatten it on the palette, so that the colours can be drawn across the surface to describe the wide areas of sunlit wall – keep the brush at a shallow angle to the surface. Switch to a small round brush to render the fine filaments of light within the shadows cast by the birdcages.

4. COLOUR, DETAIL, LIGHT

A second layer of almost tube consistency paint is applied to the sunlit walls using the round brushes. Different colours (reds, yellows and oranges) are added to the white for extra interest. Use as large a brush as possible to make the scumbling more dramatic. Any edges that are accidentally overpainted can be immediately washed away with a second damp brush. Finish off the birdcages with a Rigger, with just enough medium in the mixes to make them flow more easily. Dark accents should be painted first, followed by opaque lights and highlights, adding both white and yellow to suggest sunlight. The final dramatic shadows – in many ways the most important feature – are painted negatively. In other words, they are formed from the underpainting, around which light has been laid.

Through this exercise you will experience the full benefit of texture/modelling paste as an underpainted layer of texture. Rather than being mixed with the paint, it is applied on its own. Directional strokes are drawn directly onto the pencil drawing, achieved with a stiff nylon brush. In this way the texture can be thought of as a separate entity, allowing you to concentrate on its qualities and the structures that can be formed.

Colour, added as washes, or later as scuffs, makes this texture disclose its nature in a way that is exciting for both the painter and for the viewer. This really does add an extra dimension to the use of acrylic paints and no matter how many times this technique is employed, it will never fail to surprise and delight.

The paint is built over the texture in layers, applied from dark to light. The first washes are generally transparent, almost like watercolours. Stiffer mixes are prepared with the addition of acrylic medium, made opaque with the addition of white. Finally, glazes of colour, using acrylic gloss medium and colour, without white, add depth and richness to the underlying opaque scuffs and scumbles.

In the resultant painting, texture and colour work in harmony, seemingly indivisible and difficult to imagine as having been applied as separate layers.

Stage-by-stage

STAGE 1

Step 1 As this painting is to be rendered on a rather heavy textured surface, a sturdier ground is required, such as the canvas board used here. Use a pencil to sketch out the initial structure of the composition. The powerful silhouette of the tiger's head is carefully balanced within the rectangle and the drawing already suggests that this is to be the main area of focus within the painting. This is to be a study of camouflage and textures. The aim is to allow the tiger to emerge from the texture and colour of the background, just as it might in reality.

Once the drawing is completed, overlay it with heavy impasto textures, using texture/modelling paste, built up with a stiff bristle round brush. These strokes of paste should be structural, following the lie of the tiger's coat, the volume of its head and to suggest the flow of the background, which comprises dry vegetation. The canvas weave must be overpainted across the majority of the composition, or it will dominate and reduce the power of the subject.

By omitting colour at this stage, you can concentrate on building this structure and enjoy the physical nature of the surface.

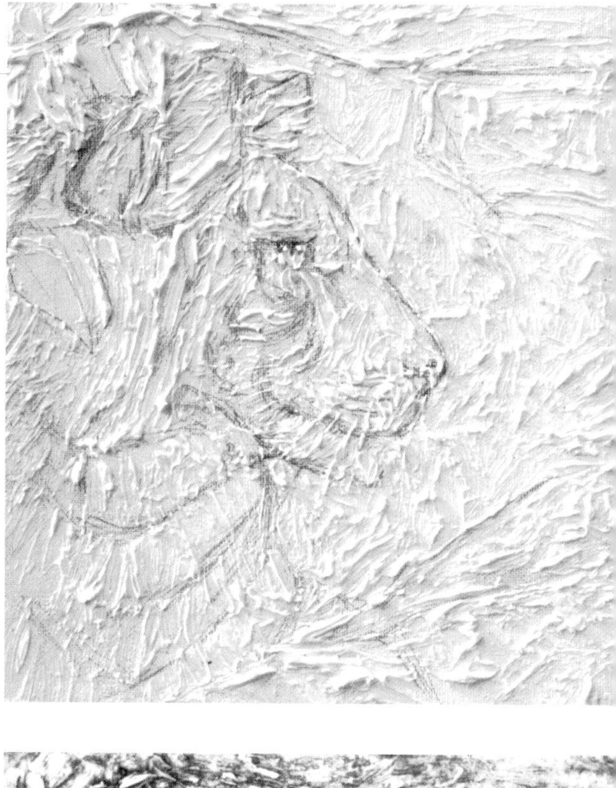

Step 2 Before going on to the paint, it is useful to visually discover the nature of the impasto texture. To facilitate this, produce a fluid mix of warm, dull yellow acrylic colour [Yo+bp+ro+TW] and gloss medium. Flood this over the surface and work into the crevices with a stiff brush. While still wet, tonk off this colour quite aggressively, using clean craft tissue paper. A piece of newsprint paper will do the job equally well at this stage, since the tonk is of a general nature. Apply even pressure throughout, using the ball of your hand. Once the paper is removed you will see that the colour has been left in the intaglio of the surface. The effect can be enhanced even further by wiping the surface gently with a clean, lint-free cloth, bringing the relief of the surface up to an even lighter value. Leave this for a few minutes to dry and then repeat the exercise, with a similarly fluid mix of dull purple [Bp+Ro+yo+TW].

These two colours are almost complementary to one another and have quite different colour temperatures. When the second colour is again tonked, the revealed layers in which the two colours visually mix are especially engaging.

A very exciting surface has now been created on which to begin the actual paint layers. All of the white has been eliminated and a textured structure constructed that will impinge its character on the overlaid colours.

NOTE

THE BOLDLY PATTERNED COAT OF THE BIG CAT HELPS ENORMOUSLY IN ACHIEVING THE CORRECT PROPORTION OF ITS HEAD. EACH STRIPE ACTS LIKE A JIGSAW SHAPED PIECE, WHICH CAN BE COMPARED TO AND SIZED AGAINST OTHER PIECES, UNTIL THE ANIMAL'S FORM IS ACCURATELY CONSTRUCTED.

STAGE 2

Generally, opaque colours are now brought into play, with white being added to the mixes. A careful balance must be achieved between filling the various areas with colour and not completely overwhelming the textures and colours beneath. In fact, underlying textures will help to break up applied brush-strokes, as long as you do not overwork the surface. Note how the undercolour is used in a subtle way for the branches. They are negatively painted, by painting the space around them, allowing the branches to be formed by the colour showing through from beneath.

Each colour is tonked immediately after application. This not only thins down the colour, but also responds to the underlying textures, which will provide unexpected and unique qualities. The more fluid the colour mix, the easier it is to lift off with a tonk.

Layers are overlaid slowly, building towards light. A cool white is added to the fur and works as a colour against the coloured greys beneath. Generally, the paint is laid more stiffly toward the head and eye and more fluidly toward the edges of the painting.

TONKING

Vary the consistency of the applied colour mixes, from thick tube consistency paint, to thin mixes with either water or medium added. Mixes containing medium are stiffer than those with water. It is essential to only paint an area that can be effectively tonked before it dries out.

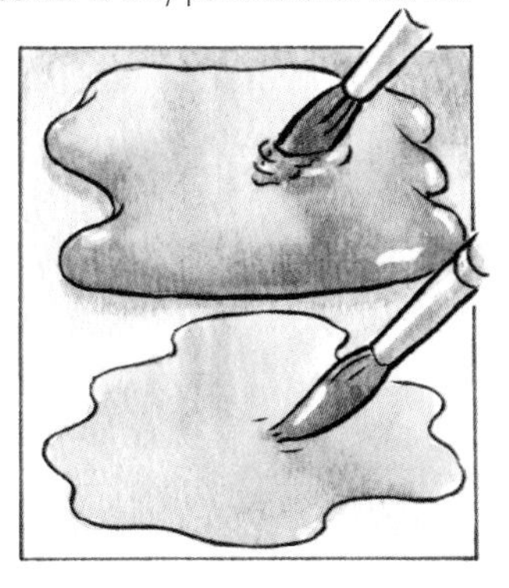

Lay a sheet of craft tissue paper or newsprint, smooth or crumpled, across the wet surface and rub down vigorously with the palm of the hand. Use a rag if you require extra pressure. On removal of the paper, the resultant textural effects are unique and exciting.

◁ **A close look at this area of background** texture reveals the layers of colour that go right back to the surface of the canvas board. The irregular lift of the paint with each successive tonk creates a quality unobtainable by ordinary brushwork – a treat for the eye and the imagination.

◁ **The final highlight to the eye** is the only point of pure white in the whole painting. That, together with the pool of colour along the bottom of the iris, creates a focal point in the painting to which everything else now appears to lead.

◁ **Between the powerful patterns** of the tiger's stripes, we can see the way the surface textures interact. In parts, the canvas texture is caught by the white scuffs. Elsewhere it is the brush-strokes, which, when scuffed, provide directional texture that best describes the lie of the animal's fur. Finally, fluid strokes applied with a Rigger ride the textures and suggest the whiskers.

STAGE 3

Up to this point, in concentrating on building the structure of the head, the tiger has become over dominant. The tiger needs to be knocked back into the background, to be camouflaged, so that it appears to emerge from the shadows. To achieve this, the surface needs rich glazes, which are again made more fluid toward the edges of the painting. These glazes bring out the underlying texture to a greater extent as they run into the crevices. They are readily lifted from the ridges by tonking, which is to continue throughout.

Thus the tiger slowly retreats back into the textures of the undergrowth, its neck and body almost disappearing to leave the strong head peeking out. The whites of the fur around the muzzle become a softer grey green and it is only the highlights of the eye that remain as a pure white, revealing the animal's life force and presence.

Common problems

PROBLEM

All paper cockles when wet, which makes it impossible to produce even brushstrokes on the surface. Cockling is due to uneven absorption of water into the paper fibres, which swell as they take up the fluid.

Solution

This is why paper is stretched when used with fluid washes of acrylic paint and it is important to have a method of stretching that will reduce the likelihood of the paper pulling away from the board when wetted.

Fig. 1 Wet the paper as evenly as possible on both sides to prevent the paper from distorting. For thin papers wet the paper with a sponge, always wet the wrong side first. Medium weight papers can be wetted under a running tap or dipped into a sink filled with water. Heavy weights should be left to soak in a bath filled with cold water for ten minutes to allow the water to penetrate through the paper fibres.

Fig. 2 To remove excess water from well-soaked paper, hold one corner and allow to drip off, then switch to opposite corner.

Fig. 3 Lay the wet paper, right side up, onto the drawing board. The drawing board used for stretching paper must be unvarnished wood. Should air bubbles be trapped under the paper, gently smooth away with your hand.

Fig. 4 Wet the gumstrip piece by piece and run through your fingers to remove excess water.

Fig. 5 Fix along edges of paper, with half on paper and half on board. Hold strip firmly at one end and push down with absorbent tissue. Overlap the tissue onto the paper, so that any gum squeezing out from underneath is picked up immediately.

Fig. 6 Ensure paper is firmly stuck by running a fingernail along the paper edge, pressing home the tape. Leave the drawing board flat, to dry evenly.

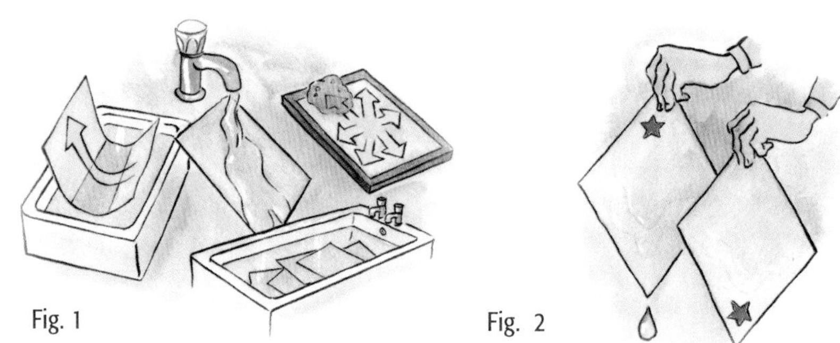

Fig. 1

Fig. 2

Fig. 3

Fig. 4

Fig. 5

NOTE

IT IS IMPORTANT TO USE GUMMED TAPE. DO NOT USE SELF-ADHESIVE PLASTICIZED PARCEL TAPE OR MASKING TAPE

TIP: A drawing board for stretching paper can be expensive. A sheet of 12mm (½") plywood will do, cut to size and sanded smooth on all four edges and both faces. To allow for the gum strip overlap the board should be 50mm (2") larger in each dimension than the size of paper most commonly used.

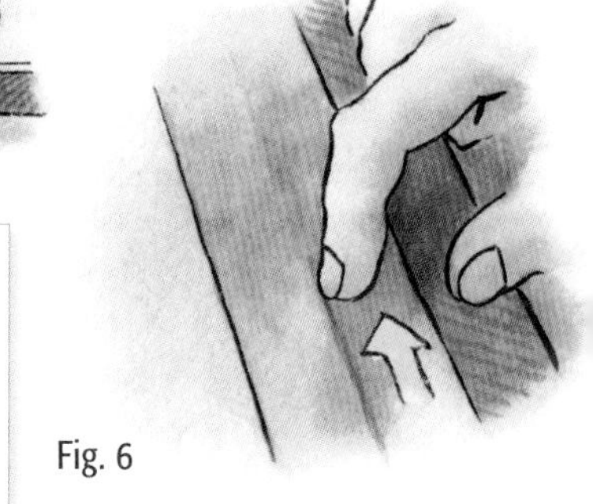

Fig. 6

Useful information

PAINTING KIT NEEDED TO COMPLETE THE TUTORIALS IN THIS BOOK

Acrylic Tube Paints (Pages 14–15)
Red-orange (Cadmium Red Deep)
Red-purple (Alizarin Crimson)
Yellow-green (Lemon or Primary Yellow)
Yellow-orange (Cadmium Yellow Deep)
Blue-green (Prussian Blue)
Blue-purple (Ultramarine)
Titanium White (TW)

Brushes (Pages 22–23)
1 x Small Round Soft Brush (e.g. Size 6)
1 x Medium Round Soft Brush (e.g. Size 8)
1 x Large Round Soft Brush (e.g. Size 10)
1 x Medium Flat Nylon Brush
2 x Nylon Riggers (1 x Size 3, 1 x Size 5)
1 x 44/50mm Hake (approx 2")
Round Bristle Brush
Round Nylon 'Bristle' Brush

Palettes (pages 28 to 35)
Stay-Wet acrylic palette (*with lidded containers for storing paint in and a large flat area for mixing colours on*)
Ceramic saucer

Surfaces (pages 36 to 43)
Watercolour Paper (Textured)
Watercolour Paper (Hot Pressed)
Canvas Paper

Acrylic Gloss Medium
Acrylic Texture/Modelling Paste
Heavy Carvable Modelling Paste
Acrylic Indian ink (Black)
Kneadable Putty Rubber
Masking Fluid (small jar)
Drawing Board
Gumstrip 50mm (2")

Acrylic Gesso Primer - White
Canvas Boards

REFERENCES
Colour Reference
Red-purple [Rp]
Red-orange [Ro]
Blue-purple [Bp]
Blue-green [Bg]
Yellow-orange [Yo]
Yellow-green [Yg]
Titanium White (TW)

COLOUR MIXING
Where the pre-fix letter is shown in capitals this denotes a larger quantity of that particular colour. Conversely, where the pre-fix letter is shown in a lower case, this denotes a smaller quantity of that particular colour.
E.G ***Bp** = **large*** amount of blue-purple
bp** = **small amount of blue-purple

Hue, Value, Tone
Hue is a bright primary or secondary colour on the basic colour circle.
Value is the degree of lightness or darkness of a colour.
Tone is the degree of lightness or darkness of a neutral grey.

Lights
The lightest hue of colour in any particular section of a painted area.
Highlights
The tiny point of light on the surface at which the light source is reflected. This reflected light maybe white, or a colour.
Accents
The darkest points of shadow of an object.
Reflected Light
The cool highlight seen within shadowed areas.
Colour Temperature
The suggestion of warmth or coolness conveyed to varying degrees by all colours.
Density of Colour
The measure of pigment carried within any paint.
Local Colour
The colour of an object under normal daylight conditions.

TERMS
Aerial Perspective
A sense of distance, usually within a landscape, caused by diminishing colour values and colour temperature.

Negative Painting
Painting the space around an object, rather than the object itself.

Arbitrary Texture
Impasto laid with multi-directional strokes unrelated to the structure or form of the subject.

Structural Texture
Impasto laid with directional strokes to suggest the structure and form of the subject.

ART WORKSHOP WITH PAUL
Tuition and Guidance for the Artist in Everyone

Log on to the artworkshopwithpaul.com website for downloadable tutorials and Art Clinic, relating to working with watercolours, oils, acrylics, pastels, drawing and other media.

Check out Paul's Bookshelf for details of all his books. Visit ***Paul's Gallery*** and the various galleries showing original paintings, limited edition prints, commissioned work, examples of collected works and work in progress.

Catch up on the latest news and details of Art Workshop With Paul Taggart Painting Breaks & Courses.

Alternatively you can write to
Art Workshop With Paul Taggart / FS
c/o Promark, Studio 282, 24 Station Square,
Inverness, Scotland, IV1 1LD

Or email
mail@artworkshopwithpaul.com

Artstrips©
Fully narrated and detailed step-by-step demonstrations form the basis of all Paul Taggart's live tutorials.

To translate these into publishable form was his ambition and thus it was that twenty years ago he conceived of the Artstrips©.

Unique to Paul Taggart, these Artstrips© are intended as a universally understood method of visually conveying detailed instructions.

Paul Taggart

Fine Artist & Author Paul Taggart

From his home in the Northern Highlands of Scotland, professional Fine Artist & Author Paul Taggart shares his enthusiasm for painting with a global audience, through the many books he has written and his extensive website. Paul Taggart's passion for art started at a very early age and ever since gaining a degree in Fine Art over thirty years ago has enjoyed the patronage of collectors, who have purchased an extensive collection of original paintings and limited edition prints.

In line with his belief that everyone should be encouraged to express themselves creatively, Paul Taggart considers it a privilege to have been able to work with aspiring artists throughout that period and to continue to do so. His aim is to provide the right sort of practical help and encouragement in a 'no-nonsense' style that makes the pursuit of painting and drawing accessible to all.

His extensive knowledge across all media in these fields proves invaluable to those following his tutorials, whether through books, the website or when attending his painting breaks and workshops.

Watercolours, oils, acrylics, pastels, drawing and mixed media – all can be developed through Paul Taggart's thorough method of tutoring, honed over many decades of listening to aspiring artists and understanding what they need to achieve their pursuit.

Art Workshop With Paul Taggart is the banner under which Paul Taggart offers a variety of learning aids, projects and events, which include books, videos, internet tutorials, painting breaks and courses.

ACKNOWLEDGEMENTS

Key people have played a major role in my life and in whom I place my unreserved trust - to them, as always, I say a heartfelt thank you. Eileen (my Life & Business Partner) and I, are delighted to dedicate this series of books to someone who has brought them to life, who wholeheartedly joined us in our work some while ago and now gets to see the fruits of her labours – Sunita Gahir. Since setting the design style for my previous series of six books, she has become an invaluable friend, both privately and professionally.

My professional life is split into painting a body of collectable originals, fulfilling commissions, producing material for books and my website, as well as tutoring aspiring painters in painting breaks etc. It is only through the continued patronage of collectors and demand for tutoring from painters that my life as a Professional Fine Artist can continue. Not forgetting those publishers with whom I share a mutual professional trust – most particularly Robert and Susan Guy of Sandcastle Books, who got this series off to a flying start.

Paul Taggart